D0064806

TWAYNE'S WORLD LEADERS SERIES

EDITORS OF THIS VOLUME

Arthur W. Brown

Baruch College, The City University of New York

and

Thomas S. Knight

Adelphi University

Structuralism

TWLS 73

STRUCTURALISM

Skepticism and Mind in the Psychological Sciences

By JUSTIN LEIBER

Massachusetts Institute of Technology

TWAYNE PUBLISHERS

A DIVISION OF G. K. HALL & CO., BOSTON

First Printing

Library of Congress Cataloging in Publication Data

Leiber, Justin.
Structuralism.

(Twayne's world leaders series ; TWLS 73)
Bibliography: pp. 139–41
Includes index.
1. Structuralism. I. Title.
B841.4.L427 149'.9 77–20136
ISBN 0–8057–7721–0

MANUFACTURED IN THE UNITED STATES OF AMERICA

Contents

About the Author

Justin Leiber is presently a visiting scientist at the Massachusetts Institute of Technology. He received his B.A. and Ph.D. from the University of Chicago and holds a graduate degree from the University of Oxford. He has been a visiting teacher at the University of Oxford and the University of London, and was a professor of philosophy at Lehman College of the City University of New York from 1968 to 1977. Mr. Leiber's publications include *Modals and Modality, Noam Chomsky: A Philosophic Overview* (Twayne Publishers and St. Martins Press), and contributions to *Analysis, Boston Studies in the Philosophy of Science, Canadian Journal of Philosophy, Philosophical Forum, Review of Metaphysics, University Review*, and other periodicals. He was born in 1938 to Fritz Leiber, science fiction and fantasy writer, and to Jonquil Stephens, poet.

Preface

Though this book is about what the labels "structural linguistics," "French structuralism," and "rationalism" label—namely, approaches to the human sciences—it is not about these labels themselves. But the labels are both misleading, symptomatic, and familiar, so I will have to say something about them.

"Structural linguistics" is the usual label for the dominant method and theory of linguistics, in the United States particularly, during the first half of this century. Leonard Bloomfield's *Language* (1933) and Zellig Harris' *Structural Linguistics* (1951) are often claimed to be the most influential general rendition of structural linguistics and its full technical culmination respectively. The "structural" part of the label may be explained in that the "structural linguists" thought the linguist should study and describe linguistic *structures*—sentences, clauses, phrases, words, word-parts, phonemes, and so on, particularly as these would be supposed to amount to classes of physical sounds in the final analysis—and not study anything "nonphysical," such as the *meaning* of sentences, words, and so on, or the logical and psychological relationships between sentences and between sentences and the world (semantics). (The reader will find full citations in the bibliography.)

Another reason for the "structural" label is the view, taken by many structural linguists, that the elements of linguistic structures are an essentially arbitrary slicing up of available vocal sounds, a grouping that makes sense only within the context of contributions to larger structures, and one which, particularly at higher levels of structure, such as sentences and semantic relationships, might mean that each such natural human language will infuse its users with a way of categorizing and understanding the world quite different from that of users of another language. Hence one finds the view that each human language is a kind of prison for its users, since there may be no way to translate

what is said in one arbitrary way of splitting up the world into another language in which the world is sectioned up quite differently.

In short, "structural linguistics" has a bias for the physical and against the mental so far as describing languages. Equally, it has insisted that aside from a few basic features of the human sound-making apparatus, there is nothing universal to human languages either in their grammar or in the system of meaning that grammatical forms convey. Those who have tried to extend the views of structural linguistics outside linguistics into philosophy and psychology have maintained these biases.

In this book I call structural linguistics and its followers in philosophy and psychology "relativistic structuralism." And I call another and more recent collection of movements in linguistics, philosophy, and psychology "universal structuralism" to emphasize opposite biases in favor of mental and universalizing explanations in these fields. The thinking that I call "universal structuralism" is often labeled "generative linguistics" when one is talking about linguistics, particularly Anglo-American linguistics. It is labeled "rationalism" or "mentalism" when people talk about some recent work in Anglo-American psychology and philosophy, and "French structuralism" or just "structuralism" when people talk about recent Continental European work in psychology (particularly anthropology) and philosophy. (I am grossly over-simplifying the Continental picture in that the European structuralists of the Nineteen Twenties and Thirties were interested in universal and psychological aspects of linguistics. In particular, the Prague school of linguistics and its Russian members, Roman Jacobson and N. Troubetzkoy, were concerned to develop a universal phonology and emphasized the relationship between linguistic theory and human cognition. Jacobson, who emigrated to the United States, has continued to deepen his concern with linguistic universal, turning Claude Levi-Strauss to linguistics as a method for anthropology and eventually becoming an elder statesman of universal structuralist linguistics. One might say that the ambiguity in Continental linguistics goes back to the turn of the century work of Ferdinande de Saussure which stressed the mental and systematic aspects

of language but also emphasized that languages are arbitrary, conventional, and wholly learned.)

Someone might object to my lumping these various movements under the label "universal structuralism." It is true that the Continental movement has had more of an impact on the arts and literature—so much so that "French structuralism" is now the or at least a fashionable style in American literary criticism. It is true that the Anglo-American form of universal structuralism, particularly under the historically apt label "rationalism," has drawn much clearer battle lines between itself and the older relativistic structuralism, while the Continental movement has been more diffuse. It will be one of the burdens of this book to justify the claim that these views belong under one label and should be treated together. I will not of course attempt to establish that in this note.

What I will say is that it is sad to label intellectual and scientific views nationally or geographically, for it suggests that the views are the prejudices and enthusiasms maintained by people steeped, and willfully or inevitably imprisoned, in one particular language and culture. It is equally unfortunate to be unwilling to extend more satisfactory labels such as "rationalism" or "mentalism" outside national or linguistic boundaries. Whether explicit or implicit, such geographical labeling suggests that intellectual and scientific views in the human sciences are the mere expression of national, cultural, or linguistic prejudices. Perhaps the tendency to such labeling and a rationale for it is the "linguistic turn" that this century has experienced in philosophy and the human sciences. Indeed, it is true that philosophy in this century has focused on language (and logic, as perhaps the general theory of meaning for language) and has seen in language the solution to traditional problems in metaphysics, ethics, the theory of knowledge, and the philosophy of science. Equally, linguistics has been seen as the most advanced and, in some ways, perhaps the most important of the human sciences, one that sets an example to the rest and one that provides a foundation for more specialized studies of cognition and culture.

Thus a relativistic structuralist might suggest that a particular language such as French (or English) breeds its own culture,

philosophy, and human sciences. But, quite recently, the conviction has grown that a deeper study of human languages, and perhaps of human cognition and culture generally, leads us to see a universal and substantial commonality to our cognitive, cultural, and linguistic nature. It is this conviction, now widely spread and impressively substantiated, that I call "universal structuralism." It is also the subject of this book, not as a mélange of fashionable movements or personalities, but—my relabeling is meant to suggest this—as a view that may be true and one that is best understood through reconstruction, examination, and criticism.

A final point. One reason I have retained the word "structuralism" is that it reminds one that views that are sometimes called "empiricism" or "behaviorism" in psychology and philosophy have derived much support from the work of the relativistic structuralists in linguistics, particularly from the period until 1960 or so, while quite different views, "rationalism" and "mentalism," have begun to flourish as in part an outgrowth of the work of universal structuralists in linguistics, particularly since the advent of transformational-generative linguistics in the last twenty years. To retain the label "structuralism" is to insist on the importance of natural language and linguistics to psychology and philosophy in this century. Were I to emphasize the labels "rationalism" and "empiricism," I would be calling attention to the way in which recent debates in the human sciences revive philosophic controversies about learning and human knowledge in the seventeenth and eighteenth centuries that did not seem to give such a prominent role to natural language and linguistics. Similarly, the use of the labels "mentalism" and "behaviorism" would emphasize a debate in late nineteenth- and twentieth-century psychology as to whether the human sciences should study the human mind or restrict themselves to the description of human behavior, to what can be seen or otherwise observed in the physical behavior of humans.

Parts of Chapter 3 derive from a paper I gave at the annual meetings of the Society for Philosophy and Psychology at Cornell University in April, 1976, that was published in the fall, 1976, issue of *Philosophical Forum.*

Preface

In writing this book I have avoided the masculine pronoun when it does not have an antecedent that is definitely of the male sex. I have read some prefaces recently in which authors have professed the principle behind this move while confessing that the practice was too difficult. After some initial difficulty, I did not find the practice troublesome. I can only conclude that those who claim that the practice is too difficult are insincere. Noam Chomsky and Stan Martens read the manuscript and made several suggestions for improving it.

JUSTIN LEIBER

Massachusetts Institute of Technology

CHAPTER 1

The Human Sciences: Questions

As the Preface suggests, this book is about two views about the human sciences in general as they derive in part from work with language. Mostly it is about universal structuralism.

But all this raises two questions immediately. Is there some substantial unity to the human sciences that makes it plausible to have views, to write books, about it? Why should linguistics or what it studies, language, be a good source for getting at this unity?

The most painfully obvious answer to the first question, and one which I will defend eventually, is that what unifies the human sciences is that they are all about human beings, all about a species of mammal whose most distinctive features, as against those of other species, would seem to be cognitive—to think; to communicate such thoughts; to build complicated devices including those that in some sense think as well; to have scientific knowledge and to manipulate nature; and so on. One might want to object that, say, human physiology or anatomy are about humans and, more generally, that that part of biology which describes human beings is "about human beings" and hence a "human science" too. The way I would want to answer this objection—and it is only a provisional answer—is to say that when the biological sciences are concerned with humans they are concerned with what processes, structures, body chemistry, and genetic and adaptive mechanisms we share with other living things. While what I am calling the human sciences—collectively, psychology; particularly, anthropology, economics, linguistics, sociology, and so on, and perhaps in some ways logic, mathematics, philosophy, and so on—are concerned with features of human beings that are not found, or found only in a very limited way, among the other things of this earth. On the

other hand, should we some day visit or be visited by intelligent creatures from another solar system, we undoubtedly might find a portion of the human sciences quite applicable to our new acquaintances.

In suggesting that the human sciences might be called, collectively, psychology, I am suggesting the sort of answer that a universal structuralist might give to our first question: what unifies the human sciences is that they are all concerned with aspects of the human mind. Further, a mind is what thinks and thinking has language as its medium: hence the centrality of linguistics. Of course, that is no answer at all until one has some idea of what the human mind, thought, and language are supposed to take in. The rest of this book will treat this topic at length, but here I would like to canvass some other answers to our first question. What else about humans might unify the human sciences? (There is no reason to think such answers are exclusive: indeed I think that there are several legitimate answers.)

Humans engage in economic activity: they are by nature productive. Marx suggested that human history has been the history of humans enmeshed in exploitive, self-propelling, and self-annihilating systems of economic activity, and that the rest of human activity, culture, and thought has been a superstructure thrown up by this basic economic foundation. Just as structuralists would understand linguistics (and perhaps logic) to have a crucial relationship to the human sciences, to psychology in general, so a Marxist might see economics to play a pivotal role, taking economic explanations to underlie those of the other sciences. It would be a mistake to think that Marxists were the first to see something like economics as the fundamental psychological science, for the founders and philosophical precursors of economics such as Thomas Hobbes and Adam Smith, as their modern counterparts, understood economics to flow from a supposed fundamental feature of human nature, namely, selfishness, or "economic rationality," as it is called today.

Whether in its ahistoric, or synchronic, form as an explanation of the mechanisms of society and justification for capitalism based on a logic of human nature, or in its Marxist historic, or diachronic, form as a similar but expanded explanation with a

derived logic of history and of human historical consciousness, large-scale economic theory has been put forward as a hard and scientific corrective to the vagaries of psychology and sociology, a science of laws based on a "realistic" theory of human (and class) economic rationality interacting on a social and technological scale. The large-scale economic theorist does not claim that economic rationality, or human and class consciousness, operate fully and directly at the level of human consciousness, nor does such a theorist generally wish to deny that humans are subject to, or think and act in terms of, other factors. What such a theorist insists on is that the larger, more dynamic, and more fundamental features of human thought and action, and of human societies through history, are explained on an economic model of rationality and consciousness.

Similarly, some have followed Rousseau (or Freud) in arguing that human origins, or untrammeled human nature—which is to say, anthropology—has a crucial part to play in the human sciences. It is not so much that anthropology as economics studies the foundational aspect of human activity. Rather anthropology studies "savage thought," to give a literal translation of the title of a work by the French anthropologist Claude Levi-Strauss. ("Savage" here meaning "natural," "elemental," unaffected by the peculiarities of some sophisticated literate human culture.)

If one wished to find the essential features of humans, it does appear natural to want to strip off recent effects of history and technology. What more natural way to think of doing this than by studying peoples who lack history and whose technology is one that has been with humans for countless centuries? Moreover, given the geographical isolation of "primitive" peoples whom the anthropologist studies, one might think that recurrent features of such people's thought and culture would not be a result of the diffusion of some idea or practice from one community to others but rather must arise from some feature of human nature.

The relationship between sociology and psychology is more global: sociology studies *human* societies, not, except as an occasional analogy, beehives, termite colonies, wolf packs, penguin rookeries, coral reefs, and so on. Equally, humans are by nature elaborately social and interdependent. One may choose

to see society as an enlargement of individual psychology; or, as Freud, one may invert such a Platonic metaphor, taking the individual mind to be a miniaturization of the social structure that confronts and shapes the child. One will want (as will the relativistic structuralist) to emphasize the sociological to the degree that one sees human beings as extraordinarily malleable creatures who are born into and wholly molded by the peculiarities and patterns of particular societies (aside from biological features more or less shared with other mammals that provide the clay for social conditioning).

To the degree that one thinks that there is much innate to human cognitive function, one will expect psychology to instruct sociology. One will see human societies in part as products of the human mind, and one will expect to discover in human societies and cultures underlying universal features that are quite distinct from what is forced on humanity by the regularities in the environment, by the uniformity in technical and material problems that face humans. Uniformities in the way human societies gather and cultivate food, for example, generally derive from the environment humans deal with and the goad of animal hunger. But when recent linguistics finds various grammatical features in all human languages, while a vast variety of other grammatical devices would seem as practical but in fact never occur, then we might expect that these universal features derive from basic features of the human mind.

In rather different ways, then, we may say that human sciences such as economics, anthropology, and sociology seek to provide some key to human cognitive nature and hence some unity or foundation for psychology, for the human sciences. To return to our second question, Why should linguistics, or what it studies, language, be a good source for getting at this unity?

To begin with language as against its study, any normal human being speaks and understands some natural language and learns to do so in essential respects quite early in life and usually without anyone providing much in the way of instruction. If one appeals to quite recent discoveries, it appears that the lateralization of the human brain (a feature that we share with some birds but not with other mammals), with specialization of language function on the left hemisphere, has been with our

ancestors for more than a million years (Isaacs, 1975). Moreover, all known languages, whether of stone-age people or industrialized societies, are equally complex and afford no distinction between the "primitive" and "advanced" language. So it seems reasonable to assume that humans have spoken languages like those found today for hundreds of thousands of years, while writing, arithmetic (in some languages one counts "one, two, three, many"), and metal working seem to have appeared only within the last few thousands of years. Further, human languages are quite complicated affairs. While it has proved quite simple to make pocket computers which will perform elementary arithmetic, it has so far proved impossible to build computers which will generate the sentences of any human language or translate the sentences of one human language into another, and this is true mostly because we do not know what sort of program such computers should be following. Indeed, linguists have only found out how truly complicated human languages are in attempting to describe the sentence structures of human languages by laying out clear, formal instructions, such as a computer could follow, for generating and describing such structures.

A simple comparison may suggest how central and startling human language acquisition is. Prior to this century few human beings knew how to read or write. Literacy usually requires several years of formal instruction. Even with more than ten years of compulsory instruction as in the United States, one finds an adult population in which over a third can hardly read the simplest text. But writing is just a way of transcribing spoken language, and reading may easily amount to no more than a process of reconverting such transcriptions into the oral language. We would think that someone knew mathematics if that person just calculated and gave answers orally, never putting pencil to paper or reading symbols. Similarly, a person who knows—and this has been the circuit of linguistic knowledge for most humans—how to speak and understand a language orally knows the essentials of that language. Indeed, modern linguists insist that languages are complete in oral form: the transcribing process is no more important to the language itself than, for example, a system like Morse code or a taping apparatus, either of which

might record the oral language in another medium. Accordingly, though any normal human being knows a human language while few have known how to read or write one, the knowledge that the human has in knowing how to speak and understand speech is of much greater complexity than that of reading and writing.

To put the matter even more abstractly, consider the human being as a kind of thinking device.

Before I proceed with this brief comparison, I will justify it in two ways against those who object to thinking of humans this way. First, remember that it would seem to be cognitive features that set humans off from the rest of nature and give some unity of subject matter to the human sciences. *How does this thing think and how does it come to do so?* seems a very fundamental question for the human sciences.

Second, to try to adopt a broader viewpoint that I will make use of later in this book, consider what might be the methodology of a scientific expedition of aliens who came to earth to study humans, supposing the aliens to have a form of biology based on silicon and oxygen but using artificial, biotechnical devices or "protoplasmic computers" composed in somewhat the same way as earth life, of chemicals such as oxygen, hydrogen, and carbon. (It might make my point more dramatically to imagine the aliens to be made of metal, but to have arisen naturally, not as creations of some other form of life. Unfortunately, while some scientists speculate that there could be a silicon-oxygen based form of natural life, it would seem biologically impossible to imagine a natural life form arising from metal. The reason, of course, that it would be more apt to imagine the aliens of metal is that we might then imagine them asking each other in metalese, "How can a machine made of hydrogen, oxygen, and carbon think?"; and they would be baffled, if not insulted, to learn that such machines could wonder whether a "mere computer," a "thinking device" made of metal, could *really* be said to *think.*)

Now suppose that the silicone-based aliens asked themselves what sort of things we were.

Suppose the question were raised as to whether humans were thinking beings. Now there is a sensible way in which the aliens could ask this question and a senseless, or unproductive, way.

We might imagine a "speciesist" alien maintaining that humans could not think because they are made of carbon, hydrogen, and oxygen. Further, this alien might speculate that the reason that humans appear to think is that they were made, at some time in the irretrievably distance past, by silicone-based (or metal-based) creatures from other planets. Now I think that the assertions of this speciesist alien would be rightly condemned by its fellow travelers as senseless and unproductive: neither the genesis, nor chemical makeup, of a thing determine whether that thing thinks. If we think, we think by nature, not by origin.

The more prudent aliens might perhaps say, given that they would understand humans as a species, as relatively similar, "Given this input, that input, and so on, or this input . . . and so on . . . and so on, the programmed [adult] versions of this kind of computer give out this output, that output, and so on, or this output . . . and so on . . . and so on. So the various versions might have any of the following range of internal, abstract programs, which could be realized physically in quite a variety of ways. But it appears obvious that these different versions just have slightly different final programs, that is, they are exposed [in childhood] to a particular variety of inputs and this process segregates these devices into versions using, at a superficial level, slightly different symbols systems. We should be able to work out what generalized learning program the immature stage must have to be able to develop into the various versions."

But, obviously, the prudent alien has to ask what sorts of capacities this sort of computing device must have to merit the title "thinking being." I think that one can give an admittedly vague but instructive answer to this question, that is, to the question as to how the aliens might validly conclude that we are thinking beings. We may ask the same question of the aliens.

What have we assumed in imagining the aliens to be intelligent? You will notice that I have made no presumptions about the physical makeup of the aliens (aside from presuming them to be silicone but that presumption is not crucial). They may have many or few legs or perhaps none at all. They may have "hearts" that circulate body fluids; maybe not. I must imagine them to have some sensory apparatus. I must also imagine them to have some means of manipulating their machines, though it

need be no more than the means which they use for communicating with each other, another feature which I must presume they possess. Thus I do suppose the aliens to have language in some sense, though undoubtedly quite different from our own. They might communicate through making and observing gestures. Or perhaps entirely through touch.

But the options are not unlimited. Their language must have something like words, grammatical rules, and sentences; and the sentences must have logical and semantic relationships, and must allow the aliens to describe the world and some of their attitudes respecting it. By "words" I mean items that are put together to form sentences. By "grammatical rules" I mean the alien's sense of what constitutes a sentence, what combinations of "words" make sentences as opposed to those that do not. By "sentences" I here mean a linguistic structure that can stand alone, that might individually and without addition express a wish, deliver an order, report a situation, ask a question, and so on. In linguistist's current usage, I am insisting merely that the alien's language will have a grammar.

I do not suppose that the aliens will do all and only the speech acts that we do—for example, they might never swear or express wishes. I do suppose that the aliens must be able to "describe the world," in that perhaps the major point of communicating is to be able to tell others how things stand where one has observed and the others have not. The "languages" of social insects, particularly bees, and gregarious mammals and birds have this general function. By supposing the aliens to be intelligent I am supposing that such descriptions in their language surpass those of nonhuman earth creatures in allowing an adequate description of nearly any sort of situation, of infinite numbers of situations. In supposing them able to "describe the world" with their language I am also surely supposing that the aliens must have some notion of negation, of contradiction, and of entailment, that is, some sentences in their language must imply the truth and falsity of others (for example, if an alien reports that Mars has two moons, the alien's sentence implies that Mars has satellites and denies that Mars has three or more satellites).

My reason for supposing that the alien's language will have

sentences *and* words and grammatical rules is derived from my supposition that the aliens, in being able to describe the world around them, will have to be able to describe an infinite number of situations. If the aliens are able to do this it would seem that they would need something on the order of an infinite number of sentences among their linguistic resources. But since each alien could not have familiarized itself, or learned, an infinite number of sentences, any more than any creature could count out the natural numbers from one to infinity, the alien must learn a (finite) vocabulary of items, "words," and must also learn how "sentences" can be constructed from these items, must possess a "grammar."

Someone may object that I am perhaps overemphasizing the descriptive and logical features of language, for indeed in taking the aliens to be intelligent I may seem to be supposing only that they are able to describe the world to each other. What of the emotional, aesthetic, expressive, and directive use of language?

I do not have any positive answer. To presume that the aliens are (at least as) intelligent as we, to suppose them to investigate the question as to whether "mere" hydrogen, oxygen, and carbon creatures are thinking beings, does seem to require that the aliens have a language of the sort sketched but does not seem to require much more. But this seems in order if one recalls that it is reasonable to regard animal "languages" we know of as allowing individuals to describe matters to others. Mammals often have a limited facial, gestural, and vocal repertoire for expressing threat or submission, rage and fear, and this sort of "language" functions in arranging questions of status among, for example, wolves and gibbons. But this is rare outside the class of mammals. Some birds sing, as some fishes signal visually, to warn off trespassers on their territory. Other birds, more social, only call to warn of trouble from predators. Many animals signal sexual readiness. On the other hand, the dance of the honey bee simply functions to tell other bees the direction and distance of food: there is presumably no need to argue with the others as to who is to go and get it, for the bluster of status competition seems to have no place among bees.

Thus one might imagine the aliens to be meticulous order-

followers who would never dream of self-expression, or gossipy anarchists who would endlessly debate every step, only acting with complete agreement, or so submerged in group goals as to act in unity without orders or debate, or as constantly engaged in status displays and conflicts. But what we cannot avoid imagining is that the aliens will have a language, a means of communication, which is a full language, not a limited sign system, in that in principle it will allow the aliens to describe to each other the infinite variety of the universe, though more particularly their home planet and locally our earth. Suppose one were to try to discover how the aliens thought and how one might communicate with them. One would need to discover their medium of communication (sound, touch, electricity, light or any of the other portions of the electromagnetic spectrum, etc.). Then one would parse it into sentences and these into words, which would amount to discovering their grammar, while at the same time one would try to establish what sentences described what situations, and so hope eventually to be able to exchange information with the aliens. In principle, what would establish for us that the aliens were persons, or thinking beings, is that we should be able to exchange our thoughts, exchange information about the world through the potentially infinite information carrying apparatus of a full-fledged language. After all, this is what establishes the same among humans from different cultures—and anthropologists report that among isolated peoples, the only word for "person" or "human" is the same as the word for members of the tribe *or speakers of its language.* Similarly, it is in effect the test that A. M. Turing proposed for determining whether a computer thinks.

It is obvious that I believe that the aliens would adopt a similar stance respecting us. That is, assuming that they did not seek to teach us their language, they would set about determining that our (primary) medium of communication is sound, more particularly the sound producible by the human vocal apparatus and capable of being heard by human ears. And, if persistent, they would determine that (within a particular speech community) various recurring groups of sounds, words, would form larger complete structures, sentences, in accord with various structural and individuating rules (in all, grammar),

while they would be able, eventually, to correlate sentences with situations, generally with those that would make them true descriptions, and with other sentences (in all, semantics). (In subsequent chapters I will fill out this very general characterization of the problem of "radical translation": at least with respect to human languages it is the central problem of linguistics.) Finally, the aliens might hope to communicate with us, particularly to exchange descriptions of parts of the universe, to share thoughts. Should this prove possible, the aliens would, so I imagine, have established that we were thinking beings, overcoming their prejudice against thinking that "mere" creatures composed of hydrogen, oxygen, and carbon could think.

In having mastered *one* of our languages (though from an alien viewpoint, as I shall later argue, all of our languages might appear dialects of one language), the aliens would be able to ask us questions, check some of our responses, and establish that we were (somewhat) logical. This process would at the same time be a way of learning our language *and* determining that we are thinking beings. What I have in mind would be that the aliens might, for example, ask "How many satellites does your planet have?" The answer, "one," in company with whole batteries of other answers, would both confirm for the aliens that we were thinkers and that they had understood our language. Similarly, series of replies such as "Twice as many" to questions such as "How many more satellites than your earth does Mars have?" would both establish for the aliens that they were understanding our language and that we were logical. Notice that the task of establishing that they understand our language goes hand in hand with that of establishing that we are thinking beings. If the aliens do not receive the answer that they expect, they will have the options of guessing that they have misunderstood our language, or that we have the facts wrong, or that we are (in this case) illogical. They will, one imagines, go on with other questions designed to determine which guess is most correct.

It is hard to think of a way of establishing that one is dealing with persons, with thinking beings, other than through the exchange of thoughts, through, in principle, a comprehensive and infinitely extendible exchange of descriptions of the universe.

And this exchange must be expressed in, realized in, some medium, some language. Of course, it would *seem* possible to imagine a creature that thought but was unable to express its thoughts to others (I wrote "*seem* possible" because I shall later consider view of philosophers such as Wittgenstein that this is really *not* possible). But such a possibility seems at best remote and irrelevant. It is to the degree that the aliens come to grasp our language, to succeed in exchanging thoughts with us in that language, that they manage to understand us as thinking beings. Equally, among the aliens and between ourselves, it is to the degree that we are able to exchange thoughts in a linguistic medium that we are able to understand one another as thinkers.

(Again it may be objected that what is central to humanity, what sets humans off from the rest of earth creatures as persons and thinking beings, is "self-consciousness," "spiritual substance," or a real or felt personal "sense of freedom and responsibility." As to "spiritual substance," which is one thing that people mean by "mind," I shall have something to say when I treat the view of Wittgenstein mentioned in the previous paragraph. As to the feeling or belief that one is "free" or "responsible" in some way that sets one apart from the rest of the material universe, I will simply say that it is obvious that many humans think that they are not "free" or "responsible" in that way. For example, the behaviorist psychologist B. F. Skinner thinks or believes just that, as one gathers from his *Beyond Freedom and Dignity*. As to whether we are *really* "free" or "responsible," whatever we may believe about it, I find it very difficult to say. The issue has been long argued and there is good reason to regard it as unanswerable in important respects. The aliens themselves might well have found it a perplexing and insoluable question: the question as to whether we were persons and thinking beings would not be such a nebulous question. As to "self-consciousness" or "self-awareness," a creature that is able to describe the world is also able to describe itself. If such a creature lacks the sense of ego, of personal anguish and existential doubt, one would not want to withhold the label "person" or "thinker." Many people attempt to attain such a state of self-lessness, and I do

not think that we would have to withdraw their status as persons and thinkers if they succeed.)

Humans are universal (that is, unspecialized) thinking devices, thinking beings, and natural language is the age-old, universal means and medium for the inculcation and interplay of this kind of existence. The reason I introduced the experiment in imagination respecting the aliens was to emphasize both these points. To ask what is central to humans, to the human sciences, may require a broad viewpoint. It is to imagine where we would stand, among the creatures there might be, not merely among the limited and arbitrary selection that this planet affords with its peculiar mix of chemicals, of temperature and seasonal variation, of evolution and accident. To conclude the thought experiment, are we not essentially more like the hypothetical aliens of silicone than we are like, for example, monkeys or moles? By the same token, though science-fiction writers imagine countless futures in which we spread through the galaxy, sampling the antelopes of Vega and the seafood of Capella among more exotic foodstuffs, no science-fiction writer has ever told a story in which we consciously eat and otherwise casually consume intelligent creatures however alien their biology or chemistry. Our moral imagination extends itself naturally to intelligent creatures. It would be wholly unnatural to imagine a space-traveled human cruelly munching a plant that could discuss the theory of relativity or compare Homer's *Iliad* to its own vegetable epics, while treating a dumb animal with the respect (how?) that we normally concede is owed a human being.

The other reason for introducing the aliens was to emphasize the centrality of language to human nature, for it is in seeing the problem from such an alien viewpoint that one realizes that understanding and translating our language would be the method, the medium and the means, for one to come to understand us as thinking beings. At the same time, while one would expect the languages of thinking beings to vary as vastly as such beings might, the peculiarities common to all human languages might reveal in an essential way what is peculiar to human thought, what is characteristic of us as a *species* of thinking being.

That is, if we say that the essential kind, or phylum, feature

of humans is that they are thinking (hence, full-fledged language using) beings, we have said at this generic level merely that humans have in common with (at least hypothetically) a vast range of thinkers only the characteristic of thinking, of being able to give comprehensive descriptions of the universe, of being able to communicate logically in a language that at least will have something like words, sentences, grammar, semantics, and some logical notions such as negation, implication, generality, and so on. The genus of generalized thinker and language user is quite broad in scope. But as with other genera, or kinds, we characterize the species—in this case, human beings—through distinctions respecting the genera or kind to which the species belongs. For example, when zoologists find a large group of animals such as vertebrates that are distinguished by a segmented spinal column terminating in a cranially encased brain, heart, gill slits, and a circulating blood system, and an internal skeleton of such and so sort, zoologists naturally subdivide vertebrates themselves in terms of such characteristics, the number of heart chambers, the specific sort of blood and respiratory system, the composition of the internal skeleton, number of vertebrae, and so on. Similarly, once one has subdivided the life development of the earth into Paleozoic, Mesozoic, and Cenozoic eras, accordingly as sea creatures, dinosaurs, and mammals were dominant large life forms, it becomes wholly natural to subdivide the Cenozoic in terms of the kinds of mammal life appearing, and so on with the rest. Again, if one breaks down human prehistory in the traditional (and perhaps misguided) way according to whether humans use no permanent tools, use stone, or use metal, it is again natural that one will further subdivide into more or less developed use of stone tools, into bronze and iron ages, and so on. In the same way, if one agrees in seeing historical humanity as economic humanity, one will subdivide human consciousness into owners and owned, lords and serfs, bourgeois and proletariat. Thus I conclude that to suppose that humans are, generically, thinking and language using beings is to suggest that in attempting to get at the essential features of humans as a species of thinking being, one should look to the peculiarities of human thought and, more particularly, of human language. We want to know

what is particular to human thought in natural language: what is universal for the human species but specific to it as one among many possible sorts of thinking beings.

The view that language (what is universal to human, or natural, language in its cognitive manifestations) is the central avenue for capturing much of what is essential and specific to humans as thinking beings is one way of understanding language (and so linguistics) to be central to the human sciences. This is the view taken by a universal structuralist such as Noam Chomsky, the primary source for the transformational-generative linguistics that has dominated the recent study of language. But there are two other reasons for understanding language and linguistics to have a central role in the human sciences, one stemming from the *methods* of linguistics and the other, more philosophical, from the seductive appeal of what has been called "the subliming of the logic" of natural language.

There is indeed a problem about the methodology of the psychological sciences, namely, how does one study "psyche," that is, mind, considering its nonsensible, or abstract, nature? There is a very old and very persistent view, termed mind-body dualism, to the effect that the world contains two quite separate kinds of things: physical bodies, which take up space and are visible, indeed, are generally open to observation with our senses, and minds, or perhaps consciousnesses, that cannot be seen or heard or touched, and so on, that have—as you are having as you read these words—thoughts, emotions, and experiences. What does seems to be true is that the psychological, or human, sciences do not study humans as would the physicist, chemist, zoologist, anatomist, or physiologist. Even the behaviorists, who vigorously deny dualism and the existence of mind, would agree that the psychological sciences do not study such matters of physical composition: rather, they study the (often conditioned or learned) *behavior,* not physical basis or constitution, of human beings.

I will try to sort out the issues between the behaviorists and mentalists in the next three chapters, but the point to be made here is that even if one says that psychology is concerned with human behavior there is still a methodological problem about the abstractness of the subject matter. Consider an ap-

parently unproblematic form of human behavior, namely, Jones utters the sentence "Flying planes can be dangerous." Now one could think of this as a straightforward set of physical events. Jones opens his mouth and out comes a string of "phonemes." First an *f* sound, then an *l*, and so on. But the facts are otherwise, as acoustical research has shown exhaustively. First, speech sound is continuous, and our sense that uttered sentences break up into discrete sounds is not physically realized; it exists only in the minds of fluent speakers of the language (humans are the creatures who are able to learn such discriminations within particular languages). Second, acoustical graphs will show that even the continuous sound periods that speakers read individual phonemes into are often physically the same as sound periods that speakers will "hear" as quite different phonemes in the context of other sentences. Third, not only do fluent speakers "hear" a major nonphysical pause between "flying planes" and "can be dangerous" because the first is the noun phrase of the sentence while the second is its verb phrase, but current linguistic research suggests that the fluent speaker "hears" in the sentence an underlying structure somewhat like *planes that are flying can be dangerous* or (the activity of) *flying planes can be dangerous*. Fourth, generally, it seems that only through an automatic, or unconscious, grasp of underlying abstract structures and grammatical processes can speakers manage to recognize (and "read in") individual speech sounds, recognize the recurrence of particular words and individuate, or recognize, occurrences of particular sentences.

Thus we, as speakers of English and as humans who *could learn*, or could have learned naturally, any human language but not vast numbers of other conceivable languages, will recognize the (abstract) sentence "Flying planes can be dangerous" and recognize the thought (proposition) that it expresses, in the peculiar accents of many different speakers of English (not to mention different printing and handwriting), in the distortions of noise, slips of the tongue, and so on. Even though two different sentences are often much more similar as literal physical sound when uttered than are two utterances of the same sentence, we will, psychologically, hear the two utterances of the same sentence as the same, cancelling the physical reality

and grasping the underlying abstraction. It is as if, whatever our individual physical chemistry, whatever, to use computer terminology, the actual hardware of our individual brains, we are all as English speakers operating with the same software, the same abstract program, the English language. When people's behavior is speaking, we understand it psychologically, which is to say abstractly, not physically and literally. It is of course because linguistics seems to have a method for capturing and describing such abstractions, such mentalistic, or cognitive, processes that it has seemed to be a model, as a science, for the rest of the human sciences.

But the abstractions of human behavior, while most dramatically and comprehensively apparent in language activity, is present everywhere we look at human behavior, at human activity within human cultures and institutions. While, for example, the gestures and expressions that accompany speech are less abstract and less complicated, they do exist at a level of psychological reality quite distinct from literal physical occurrence. While something physically tantamount to a smile is a friendly bit of gestural behavior among most peoples (but not all by any means), what is a submissive and slightly embarrassed grimace in one culture or status relationship can mean a hearty welcome in another, or an empty conventional greeting in a third. Similarly, what North American male may find an appropriate and friendly body distance for a face-to-face business conference may seem so distant as to suggest coldness and unfriendliness to a South American businessman. For most North American city blacks, during a face-to-face conversation, it is normal and friendly for speaker to keep an eye on the hearer but not as much the other way around, while the reverse is true for most North American whites; and both may be disconcerted by the normal attentive British style which is for both speaker and hearer to maintain eye contact most of the time.

We are perhaps most conscious of the fact that human behavior is abstract (has a mentalistic character) in the case of what we regard as explicit ceremonies and rituals, actions that achieve effect only against a network of social conventions: christening, contracting, betting, marrying, oath taking, sentencing, vowing, and so on. To emphasize the verbal and performance

character of a crucial part of such activities, philosophers sometimes refer to such matters as performatives, as speech acts.

But, particularly as we stand back from our own culture, or consider as the anthropologist cultures quite different from our own, we realize that most human behavior, and not only such activity but the objects humans use or describe, are invested with meaning and must be understood abstractly. This is not too hard to see respecting artifacts. To give a representative example, chess pieces are literal physical objects, but to understand them that way is not to understand them at all. From the viewpoint of literal physical reality there are countless chess pieces of all composition, shapes, and sizes. From the abstract viewpoint of the game of chess, there is just the thirty-two black and white pieces and the sixty-four square board (the pieces and board need not even be physically real, needing neither physical shape nor spacial dimension, for a properly programmed computer—or a human mind—can play a game internally). The white king, for example, may be represented by wood, metal, plastic, and paper in all shapes and sizes, just as the number two may be represented by varied expressions, by print, writing, sound in different symbolisms and languages. But there is only one white king just as there is only one number three and what defines the white king is its abstract, rule-governed, or structural relationships to the other pieces and to the game, its power of movement and significance, whatever may happen to its physical representations (the white king, for example, can never be captured, just as the number three cannot be divided evenly by any other natural number, though of course someone can grab the wooden representative off the board and run away with it, just as someone can neatly cut in half a slip of paper with "3" written on it). I shall return to the chess analogy in the concluding chapter.

As in the case of games, so with artifacts generally it is the sense that we assign objects, or the abstractions we read into them, within a pattern of meanings, that confronts the human sciences with methodological issues. Thus if one were to discover a rock formation or a tree that, through some freak of nature, had acquired the shape and dimensions of a typical chair, one would be reluctant nonetheless to say that it is a chair,

because one understands a chair to be something intended for sitting, an abstract feature which humans assign, not natural accident. So it is with artifacts in general.

The anthropologist Claude Levi-Strauss plausibly maintains that we also invest natural objects with meaning. The human mind, sometimes in universal aspects, sometimes in accord with the adjustments of particular human cultures, thinks in, assigns sense and structure to, nature itself. Indeed, Levi-Strauss, marshalling the results of many researchers, shows that so-called "primitive" humans create enormously complicated classifications and descriptions of countless plants and animals quite apart from any more practical interest than abstract curiosity, and one sees recurring features and relationships in these classifications, and the myths that reveal them, that may reveal the abstract character of the human mind as it attempts to structure and understand the world about it. Levi-Strauss straightforwardly tries to use the terminology and methods of linguistics in his endeavor.

In his latest and most massive work, *Mythologiques,* for example, Levi-Strauss attempts to isolate minimal items, "mythemes," that are joined with others to make up the structure of myths within and among different cultures, while at the same time uncovering "transformational rule" relationships between such myths (that is, global rules that show what combinations of mythemes may or may not be possible quite apart from what combinations have actually been found). Levi-Strauss analogizes his undertaking to that of an observer at fortune-telling sessions who can observe the clients and have various facts about them, and who can record the fortunes that are told them, without however being permitted to see the pack of cards or know anything directly about it. One gathers that the clients are analogous to the objective situations faced by those who create the myths (that is, the fortunes). The problem for the anthropologist, for mentalist psychology generally, is to discover what the pack of playing cards that the fortune-teller uses consists in, that is, how many cards and what formal relationships (Levi-Strauss, 1955, in De George). While Levi-Strauss sometimes maintains that such methods are particularly likely to elicit the structure of mind in that in myths we find

creativity at free play, quite detached from the pressure of material need, he believes that the peculiarities of the human mind are everywhere at work,

> From words the linguist extracts the phonetic reality of the phoneme; and from the phoneme he extracts the logical reality of distinctive features. And when he has found in several languages the same phonemes or the use of the same pairs of oppositions, he does not compare individually distinct entities. . . . The transition from conscious to unconscious is associated with progress from the specific toward the general. In anthropology, as in linguistics, therefore, it is not comparison that supports generalization, but the other way around. If, as we believe to be the case, the unconscious activity of the mind consists in imposing forms upon content, and if these forms are fundamentally the same for all minds—ancient and modern, primitive and civilized—it is necessary and sufficient to grasp the unconscious structure underlying each institution and each custom, in order to obtain a principle of interpretation valid for other institutions and other customs. (Levi-Strauss, 1963, p. 20)

At this point I wish merely to raise questions for subsequent chapters. Are there conceptual and cultural universals both respecting human language and more generally? Does it make important sense to say that historical sensitivities, cultures, and institutions are a selection from humanly possible as opposed to humanly impossible sensitivities, cultures, and institutions? Or is each human culture, each institution, a unique historical accident apart from those characteristics which stem directly from biological drives and features we share with animals?

Are the methods of the linguist particularly appropriate for the human sciences in general? Or are such methods unique to the study of language in a narrow sense, allowing only vague and dubious analogous extensions to the other human sciences?

CHAPTER 2

Philosophical Skepticism and the Human Sciences

I will commence this chapter by raising the distinctively philosophical issue characterized earlier as "the subliming of the logic of natural language." What I have in mind are three linked tendencies in the twentieth century "linguistic turn" in philosophy: (1) the view that *all* philosophical, conceptual, and theoretical questions are questions of linguistic analysis, of the philosophy of language; (2) the view that, deep down in a theoretical understanding, a natural language—as any language—is best understood as in effect a theory of reality and a logical system (in fact the theory and logic that its speakers share); and (3) the view that denies that humans should be regarded as having thoughts which may be expressed in one natural language or another, denies that the test of a good translation is that the same thought is expressed in two languages, just as it denies that sameness of meaning within a language is to be taken as a question of whether the same thought, or proposition, is expressed by two sentences. Thus human thought and its logic is always strongly relative to a particular human, or artificial, language and may inculcate, if not imprison its speakers within, a unique and peculiar sectioning up of reality.

The first view is specifically associated with logical empiricism, with the view that all that we say about the world that is cognitively meaningful, that is true or false, consists of either synthetical or analytical sentences. Familiarly, synthetical sentences make particular factual statements about the world and are confirmed (or falsified) by empirical investigation, by observation and experiment by scientists or others. In being neither theoretical or conceptual, such synthetical sentences do

not state what is possible or necessary; they simply assert particular, contingent facts or conjunctions of such. On the other hand, analytical sentences, which are basic to logical, mathematical, philosophical, and theoretical discourse, do show us conceptual truths concerning what is possible or necessary, but such "truths" are not so much truths about the world (for they cannot be false) as they reveal or are a by-product of our linguistic conventions, of our determination to use a language and its symbols in a consistent way.

The view that all philosophical, conceptual, and theoretical truths are a by-product of the conventions of our language is an ancient, tenacious, and polymorphous view. Ancient because it can be traced back through the eighteenth-century empiricist arguments of George Berkeley and David Hume against abstract ideas or entities to the nominalists of the Middle Ages and beyond them to the beginnings of philosophical and scientific thought. Tenacious because it is still very much alive in diverse forms, though its revival at the turn of the century in attacks by mathematical logicians on "psychologism," on the claim that logical and mathematical truths derive from human psychology, and still more recently by the logicial empiricists, has suffered much in the way of refutation and retrenchment. Polymorphous because the view—at least in the loose formulation in the first sentence of this paragraph—may be maintained by philosophers, psychologists, and linguists with radically different interpretations of what the view entails.

One strand in the view I am sketching is the attempt, sometimes though misleadingly associated with Bertrand Russell's and Alfred North Whitehead's *Principia Mathematica,* to show that the truths of mathematics and of logic itself follow from a small group of logical axioms that might be described as linguistic conventions (strictly, this view is most accurately ascribed to logical empiricism). Thus the most general theoretical or conceptual truths, those of logic and mathematics, are claimed to follow from purely formal, or "syntactical," conventions of our language, while other theoretical or conceptual truths result, for at least some logical empiricists, from the special vocabulary conventions of particular sciences or from the ordinary vocabulary of everyday life. To give some familiar examples of these

four categories, the following have been regarded as equally conventional and analytic truths: "A sentence follows from its double negation" (more compactly, "If not [not p], then p"); "$5 + 7 = 12$"; "Heat is the motion of molecular particles"; "All bachelors are unmarried males."

The view that all theoretical or conceptual truths are conventional and analytical has had its problems, and has shifted emphasis for some empiricists to something more like the second view, namely, that while all theoretical and conceptual truths are linguistic, language itself is a kind of theory of reality. One problem in the view that all mathematical truths are conventional, following from some stipulated axioms, is that it is possible to show that all the truths of arithmetic do not follow within any language from any consistent, recursive, finite set of first-order axioms whatsoever: rather than being purely formal, or "syntactical," the truths of mathematics would seem to depend, semantically, on the reality to which mathematics refers. Another problem is that the theoretical or conceptual truths of science do not seem to be arbitrary verbal stipulations as "cranium" is a learned replacement for "brainpan." For example, "Heat is the motion of molecular particles" seems on the one hand to be a discovery and not a verbal stipulation; and it also seems to be a *necessary* truth of thermodynamics. Indeed, as I shall attempt to show in Chapter 3, the central theoretical generalizations of current linguistics have a similar status. On the other hand, that every bachelor is indeed an unmarried male does seem to be a straightforward consequence of linguistic convention, part of what a competent speaker of English learns in learning English, and not in discovering facts or establishing theories about the world to which English allows us to refer.

But there is a more comprehensive problem about the view that all philosophical, conceptual, and theoretical truths are a by-product of linguistic convention (or, for that matter, the second view that our language is a theory of reality, a view which may be considered, historically, a retrenching reaction to criticisms of the first view). The problem begins in asking *what language (or languages) are we talking about?* (Parenthetically, a natural answer would be "Natural languages such as English," to which it might be added, "and the linguists are

those scientists who would best answer the question as to what semantics or logic, hence what theoretical or conceptual truths, might be contained in the linguistic scientist's characterization of natural language, of the linguistic competence belonging to the fluent native speaker of natural language or of some particular natural language." However, linguistics as a science, and as one that might entertain such questions, is a development of the last few decades and many still feel that they can describe the relevant characteristics of natural languages while practically ignoring scientific linguistics. Thus let us return to the question *what language [or languages] are we talking about?* without immediately introducing such an answer.)

Historically, there has been a strong and a weak answer to our question. The strong answer is *whatever natural language you happen to be speaking*—in our case, English. The seemingly weak answer is *the simplest logical language into which we can translate the significant portions of empirical science, mathematics, and most everyday factual talk that take place in natural language.* The trouble with the weak answer is twofold. Either it is a tactical maneuver, an attempt to maintain the strong answer through arguing that whatever apparent theoretical or conceptual distinctions or truths cannot appear in translation into a favored logical language have no sense and hence could not in actuality have been theoretical or conceptual distinctions or truths in natural language (as in Quine, 1960). Or there is no way of establishing that the "translation" has not eliminated important theoretical and conceptual matter, if not wholly distorting the logic of natural language; for, after all, our theoretical and conceptual problems are expressed and argued in natural language (and even when they take place in special symbolisms, ancilliaries to natural language, for these symbolisms—indeed logical languages themselves—had to be explained originally, to those that learned them, through translation into a natural language that they knew already). Accordingly, I shall consider the strong answer, namely, in full, that all philosophical, conceptual, and theoretical questions are questions of the linguistic analysis of *natural language*, of in our case, *English.*

It is in certain respects clear what is meant by the vocabulary, syntax, and semantics of an artificial language such as, for ex-

ample, a sentential logic. A logician stipulates a vocabulary (p', p'', p''', p'''', and so on, *not, or, and, if then, if and only if*—I am using the words rather than the logical symbols but the meaning of these items will be given wholly within the logical language so they will not depend on English). The logician gives for this vocabulary a recursive criterion that determines what is to count as a well-formed formula, that is, a sentence, of the language (using A' and A'' for any well-formed formula created by these rules, if A' is p', p'', p''', p'''' or p^n, it is well-formed; *not* A' is well-formed; A' *or* A'' is well-formed; A' *and* A'' is well-formed; *if* A' *then* A'' is well-formed; and A' *if and only* A'' is well-formed). The logician can then proceed to give axioms and rules of inference providing a proof procedure for establishing all the logical truths the logician wants, consistently, and for determining that certain inferences are truth-preserving, or the logician can give some semantic procedure for establishing that formulas are logical truths or that certain arguments are truth-preserving. In a sense the only direct criticism that can be made when one attempts to construct such logical languages is that one has created an inconsistent system, one that allows a contradiction to be derived (either because the inference procedures allow such a derivation in themselves or because the formation rules allow paradoxical sentences).

But what is involved in characterizing a natural language such as English seems quite different. English does have a vocabulary, one that is specified loosely in a dictionary and more circumspectly in the abstract "lexicon" of a systematic linguistic description of a language within a generative grammar. Similarly, there are a potentially infinite number of English sentences composed from this vocabulary with appropriate "bracketing" or parsing (that is, the well-formed formulas or grammatical sentences of English). The linguist seeks to provide a criterion of well-formedness in giving the rules of English syntax, in specifying the generative grammar that will generate and structurally describe all and only the sentences of English.

But of course the linguist does not stipulate the vocabulary of English, nor does the linguist stipulate what are the potentially infinite set of grammatical English sentences, nor does the linguist stipulate the structural descriptions of these sentences,

nor does the linguist stipulate the rules of English syntax at least up to a certain indeterminacy. (That is, in specifying the abstract generative device that generates English sentences with appropriate structural descriptions, the linguist is attempting to describe something internalized in the fluent speaker of English, something whose indeterminacy is convergently reduced in that it was learnable by a human in normal development and contains many universal features indigenous to the human mind, to human language acquisition.) The linguist, in brief, is describing what is there, not stipulating a vocabulary and a criterion of well-formedness and so a set of sentences. If what the linguist says is there is not there, then the linguist is wrong.

In general, if native speakers do not have a word or a sentence as part of English, then it is not part of English, whatever the linguist may say. Again, though more subtle tests may be required, if native speaker's intuitions about the structure of English sentences disagree with those of the linguist, the linguist is wrong. Nor may the linguist respond by claiming that the native speakers are inconsistent or uneconomical. The linguist is not to tell the native speakers how they should speak. Further, if, as the logician Alfred Tarski claimed to show, there are grammatical but logically paradoxical sentences in natural language, sentences whose utterance seems to have to be both true and false, then it is not the business of the linguist to demand the reform of natural language as a logician would rightly condemn a "logical" language in which such sentences could be found (Tarski, 1956). The linguist is not out to "sublime" the syntax of ordinary language.

Of course, the linguist cannot ask the native speaker for the particular and universal rules of English syntax (for what would correspond to the logician's rules specifying well-formedness given on page 37, though these rules are quite arbitrary among logicians). While native speakers of English have clear-cut and convergent judgments about which words and sentence structures are English, they have no conscious knowledge of the abstract principles and processes, the general rules, that generate English sentences. For, to repeat one of the remarks I quoted from Levi-Strauss, "The transition from conscious to unconscious is associated with progress from the specific to the general." Since

the fluent speaker-hearer is in command of a potentially infinite body of sentences, hearing and uttering new sentences continually, the speaker-hearer must somehow internalize an unconscious knowledge of generative rules. In Chapter 3 I will examine the degree to which such rules can be determinate, but there can be little doubt that there must be such rules, the more universal ones particularly revealing abstract mental structure. Thus again the linguist does not purport to stipulate whatever will generate the desired set of structures; rather, the linguist purports to describe what is there.

Indeed, a natural language such as English not only has a syntax but also a semantics. That is, the native speaker has systematic and lexical intuitions about meaning, about the logical relationships between sentences (lexical intuitions about synonymy and antonomy among words and more systematic intuitions about sameness of meaning, logical implication, and inconsistency among sentences and so on). These intuitions would correspond—very roughly however—to the logical truths and implications that the logician would determine through proof or semantic rules. Certainly, the native speaker's intuitions about semantics often have a direct relationship to syntax and in any case can be accommodated to a considerable degree in the linguist's full systematic characterization of the native speaker-hearer's linguistic competence, of the linguistic characterization of English. However, again, the linguist describes what is, and attempts to describe systematically the ordinary fluent native speaker-hearer's intuitions about semantics, not to improve these intuitions, or to simplify them, regiment them, or render them sublime. The linguist has no business quarreling with the native speaker's intuitions about logical truths, sameness of meaning, inconsistency, and implication, any more than the linguist can quarrel with the native speaker's intuitions about wordhood or sentencehood. The linguist's principle is neutrality, particularly where there are real and not narrowly grammatical differences among speakers, though the linguist may let the system decide where it is not clear that native speakers have any intuitions at all.

Of course, the systematic generative linguist does not literally describe everything that speakers do. The linguist describes *the competent* speaker-hearer of English and the linguist is

idealizing or abstracting in that sense. Thus the linguist is not describing any particular group of English speakers such as the highly educated or extremely logical, nor those with specialized training or vocabulary. Linguists do describe dialects of English such as Southern or Down Mainer, but the speech of the "well-informed," the "scientific," any more than that of the good, truthful, or beautiful, is not a dialect, not a properly linguistic notion, because an inappropriate notion of competence is being introduced. Thus the linguist wishes to systematize the intuitions of nearly all or most speakers, and if such intuitions clash, the prudent linguist will preserve a neutrality in characterizing the language. This is particularly necessary when the clash is not a matter of untutored and unreflective linguistic intuition but one involving debated logical, theoretical, conceptual, or factual issues. Since competency in general or theoretical knowledge appears in how one so endowed speaks, or listens, the prudent linguist has of course no business purporting to describe how the *competent* physicist, philosopher, logician, mathematician, biologist, geologist, historian, etc., speaks. (If the linguist did have such a task, it would be endless and all-encompassing, for there would be no science but linguistics.) Rather, the linguist aims at describing abstractly, and so respecting *linguistic competence*, how the native speaker-hearer speaks apart from accident, slips of the tongue, simple limitations of memory or pronunciation, and quite apart from what influences on speech derive from theoretical and specific knowledge of the world, from all nonlinguistic competencies.

In particular, though some have indeed claimed as a logical truth that a sentence follows from its double negation (that "If not [not *p*], then *p*"), the prudent linguist would not want to make this principle part of the semantics of English (or any other natural language, for example, Dutch). Why? Because some logicians and philosophical mathematicians, the intuitionists, believe that it is not a logical truth, both that it is not their habit to employ this principle, and that it is not one that they think should be employed, on peril of incoherence, respecting things that we cannot in principle exhaustively survey. Are all logical (theoretical, philosophical, conceptual, and mathematical) truths analytically true as a matter of the semantics

(or semantic conventions) provided by the linguist's adequate linguistic characterization of English (or any other natural language)? If the answer is "yes," then the fluent speaker of English (or other natural language) should find it unreflectively and obviously true that "All logical (theoretical, philosophical, conceptual, mathematical) truths are analytically true" in just the way that such a fluent speaker would find it unreflectively and obviously true that "If it's raining, then it's raining." But, in fact, few speakers, fluent or otherwise, of English (similarly for other languages) find the former sentence unreflectively and obviously true—either true analytically as a matter of the linguistic competence, which it must be if the thesis is to hold, or true at all. Indeed, if one were to find a natural language whose speakers agreed that it was trivially and analytically true that "All logical (theoretical, philosophical, conceptual, mathematical) truths are analytically true," taking this sentence as translated into their language, one could only conclude that all the speakers of the language in question were logical empiricists, that is, adherents of a contentious philosophical doctrine, for it is a feature of an adequate translation of a sentence such as "All logical (theoretical, philosophical, conceptual, mathematical) truths are analytically true" that the translation should preserve the obvious fact that it propounds a contentious and broadly philosophical doctrine.

Another and more general way to put the argument of the previous sentence would be as follows. Most general and serious scientific, philosophical, theoretical, conceptual, logical, and mathematical issues are issues for a relatively small group of individuals who are not sectioned off from the rest of humanity in speaking a particular natural language or dialect of a natural language, for indeed they speak, and discuss the issues that distinguish them as a group, in many different languages. What distinguishes such groups are not distinctions primary and essential to linguistics. Mathematics, philosophy, geology and theoretical physics, for example, are not four "dialects" of English or any other natural language, for one can carry on these undertakings in many different natural languages, even concurrently. The propositions and theoretical understandings that characterize such undertakings do not belong to any particular

natural language. If natural languages are "prisons," they do not hold such inmates. We cannot, and do not, find such discussions confined in principle or even with rare exceptions in fact to speakers of some particular natural language.

Respecting the "subliming of the logic of natural language," I conclude negatively. *No* philosophical, conceptual, or theoretical questions are questions that will be resolved in the linguist's adequate characterization of the semantics and syntax of a natural language, of the semantic, syntactic, and phonological characterizations of particular sentences. Of course, the theoretical discoveries and generalizations of linguistic science are quite another matter. I think that they are important both for philosophy and psychology. But the linguist does not proceed by stating linguistic theories in English sentences and then asking whether the ordinary (that is, the nonlinguist) competent English speaker will find them true. The linguist may believe, for example, the theoretical generalization expressed by the sentence "English is not a finite state language," but the linguist does not consult the intuition of the native speaker about this sentence to find out whether it is true. Linguistics has much to tell us about human psychology but not by characterizing particular sentences in which human psychology (philosophy, science, etc.) are mentioned. Linguistics impinges on psychological and philosophical theories when linguistics is most theoretical and general, not in the parsing of a few English sentences.

I also conclude that a natural language as characterized by a linguist is not a theory of reality. It cannot be wrong or right in the relevant way, for it is the medium within which we must understand theorizing and theoretical disagreement to take place, not a straightjacket that excludes such. Any sentence of English (or another natural language) which expresses a theory and about which some theoreticians who speak the language disagree, have disagreed, or might disagree, cannot be clearly true or clearly false in the idealization of *the* competent speaker-hearer. By speaking of *the* competent speaker-hearer we intend of course an idealization that abstracts from such disagreements and maintains neutrality, not one that decides such disagreements.

I will return to the question as to whether our native language imprisons us in its own metaphysic, making "radical

translation" impossible beyond certain severe behavioristic limitations—whether, which comes to the same, it is but an empty figure of speech to speak of thoughts or propositions apart from the use of sentences of our particular language. Indeed, it is in the technical and theoretical development of transformational-generative grammar, a move from the dominance of relativistic structuralism to universal structuralism within syntactical theory itself, that we will find the best reasons for rejecting the prison thesis and for maintaining that "radical translation" allows and demands more than a behaviorist and nominalist theory of language and thought.

One final point. People ask whether a natural language is very like or very different from the artificial languages that logicians, mathematicians, and theory builders construct. If one takes the comparison seriously, one must of course agree that the linguist can only be regarded as describing a system and one that does not belong to the linguist; the linguist is obviously not constructing or correcting a system. One could then analogize the linguist's task to that of someone, call this person the "formal linguist," who is trying to discover and describe what formal language, what logic, is being employed by one or more of the following: (1) a group of mathematicians at a conference on topology or analysis, supposing them, mostly, to write logical and mathematical symbols on blackboards and use verbal equivalents (they would say "wedge" for the logical symbol "v," "squiggle" for "∼," "horseshoe" for "⊃," thus avoiding the English words "or," "not," "if ——, then ——," and so on; (2) a group of students in a classroom who are being drilled in using a logical notation for predicate logic (assuming as in [1] that they avoid using a natural language—perhaps the instructor has sworn them to this for severe pedagogic reasons); and (3) suppose the "formal linguist" is "describing" a formal language, a specially refined personal symbolism, that the formal linguist speaks *when being consistently logical.*

Now I think that insofar as the analogy between an artificial language and a natural language holds, the formal linguist most approaches the "natural" linguist in case (1). Note that I am assuming that the group of mathematicians are not directly concerned with their logical language, for they are talking about

topology and real numbers. I presume that the mathematicians will make "performance" slips: routine little errors that will be ignored as trivial or quickly corrected as with speakers of a natural language. But the mathematicians will have somewhat differing notions of proof and of the sense of logical symbols (for example, some might be intuitionists or some sort of constructivists while others might be platonists, etc.).

Contradictions might be derived if one took all the arguments that any of these mathematicians accepted and jammed them together. One might then say that these mathematicians were speaking different languages. But they are *communicating*, and they *disagree* about whether certain inferences are good ones. This is of course the situation in natural language. One might want to be strict about the mathematicians and their uses of symbols. One might say, "different rules of inference, different languages; different views about consistency, proof, or the sense of any logical particle, then different languages; inconsistency or logical paradox, then no language at all." Thus is the logic of a common language "sublimed"; and thus also we assimilate (1) to situation (3). But this is not the case with natural languages, which are spoken by persons with differing theoretical, logical, and conceptual views. Nor is it true in the sense that the mathematicians at the conference are communicating in a common language: they understand each other which is a reasonable test of commonality of language. The situation in a natural language and in (1) has these fundamental common features: there is a community of speakers; there are theoretical, conceptual, and logical disputes among speakers, and within limits there is no official set of rules (as there is in [2]); and while there are routine common practices that allow a competence-performance distinction, there is a wholly distinct sense in which the participants hope to make *discoveries* about a subject matter—in this case mathematical structures and sequences—that exists independently of what the current rudimentary common denominator of acceptable practice amounts to, discoveries that may lead to new ways of using symbols.

Similarly, linguists can make discoveries, can establish new theoretical generalizations about psychology and language, ones which may eventually have some effect on the way linguists

speak or even on the semantic and syntactical intuitions of ordinary fluent speakers. It will not do to say that this was really the way we were speaking (thinking, reasoning) all along. To prospectively read the discoveries of the future into the present and past must be wrong, for then we can never describe the present or the past. To say that the way we speak (think, reason) cannot be wrong is to embrace the worst sort of psychologism. It is also to make empirical theories of mind and language impossible, for it fails to distinguish science, including theoretical linguistics, mathematics, and logic from the study of the peculiarities, even as broad as our species, of human mind, human thought, and human language. We must be able to speak better; otherwise, what is a future for?

The second point with which I would conclude this chapter has to do with the possible incoherence of the notion of a personal, or private, language. I here have in mind a genuinely private, full-fledged language, not a cipher or "secret writing" for an ordinary public language as one might cipher by substituting the next letter in the alphabet for each letter in some English sentence or conceal some Italian sentences in the manner of Leonardo da Vinci by writing them while looking through a mirror at one's writing surface. In effect, I raised the issue of the impossibility of a genuinely private language on page 24 when I mentioned the possibility of a creature that thought but was unable—not unwillingly or momentarily indisposed—to express its thoughts to others. Since it is sometimes supposed that such a hypothetical being with an essentially private language or manner of thinking would have to be a nonmaterial substance, or that such a disembodied mind could only have such a language, one cannot raise this issue without calling into question the relationship between mind and its study, psychology, and matter and the physical sciences. Indeed, philosophers such as Wittgenstein have wanted to argue that a private language is impossible, an illusion produced by an incoherent "subliming" of certain features of ordinary public languages, because some philosophers have maintained, solipsistically, that the individual may learn and understand language in terms of personal sensory and mental experience, coherently leaving open the question of

whether or not the external physical world and other consciousnesses actually exist.

In terms of the history of philosophy, the argument that an essentially private language is impossible and incoherent is an argument against solipsism. It is equally an argument against the view that someone understands the meaning of nouns, verbs, adjectives, and so on, by associating them with particular kinds of personal, or phenomenal, experiences—inner sensations, feelings, images, and so on, generally what is immediately accessible to the individual consciousness but not in any way to others except through the individual's reports or through inferences from the individual's behavior. The solipsist view that it is possible that only I exist, or that I do not know that anything (or anyone) exists beyond the immediate data of my own consciousness, is only interesting if I can know that I exist or know that the data on my consciousness exists.

The classical solipsist could be understood to reason as follows.

I am conscious of various phenomenal data—experiences of colors, shapes, smells, tastes, sounds. And I know that I have these personal "inner" experiences. I had believed unreflectively that there are other human minds with such experiences and an external world of objects and causal processes that give rise to these experiences in me. But my belief in a material world and other minds can only be an inference from what I do know, from the data of my experience. And when I ask myself about the worth of this inference, I realize that the world external to my private experience may not exist or be wholly different from what I suppose. Indeed, it may be that I cannot have even the slightest evidence that anything beyond my experience exists, for what can evidence be but experiences of mine, and no regularities in my experience can give me any basis for believing anything whatever about matters outside my experience. I may "believe" that various things outside my experience cause my experiences; but since I can never establish the existence of something outside my experience, so as to begin to ask whether this sort of thing is regularly accompanied by some sort of experience in me, my "beliefs" about the external world are

wholly unverifiable. These "beliefs" lack any real meaning for me since meaning for me is a matter of my experiences.

Modern solipsism may be understood as the same line of thought put into explicitly linguistic terms. Thus the modern solipsist might reason as follows.

I can describe to myself, or put into sentences that I can understand, the various phenomenal data of my consciousness. I can issue sentences to myself that state my private, introspective experiences of color, shape, smell, taste, and sound. And usually I can also say to myself truthfully that I know that I have the particular experiences that I describe. Quite apart from such descriptions of inner experience, I had thought that I could issue sentences to myself that describe other minds with experiences like mine and an external world of objects and causal processes that give rise to these experiences in me (indeed, I had thought that these inner experiences were my evidence, my basis for belief in, the sentences of mine that describe the character of these external objects). But reflection teaches me that insofar as I can know what I mean by sentences about external objects, these "external object sentences" cannot for me mean anything more than that I have or will have various mental experiences, that my "external objects sentences" can mean for me nothing more than some collection of sentences about my possible mental experiences. More specifically, I can think to myself and know what I mean by phenomenal sentences such as "I am now conscious of a yellowish blotch," "There just was a ticklish feeling," "The tune 'rump-titty-tum-ta-tee' is running through my mind," and so on. But when I reflect on what the external object sentence "There is a bar of sulphur in the right-hand drawer of the dark mahogany desk in front of me" means to me, I realize that it can only mean (in my private language) some indefinite list of sentences such as "If I feel such and so 'impressions of muscular activity in my right arm and fingers' and feel such and so 'impressions of the sound of wood scraping on wood,' then I will have the 'impression of a yellowish rectangular shape against a dark brown background' in the lower right-hand portion of my visual field," "If the 'impression of a yellowish rectangular shape occupies an increasingly large portion of my visual field,' I will have 'an

impression of an acrid, breath-taking odor,'" and so on. Thus I can only understand each external object sentence to mean some indefinite conjunction of conditional sentences about my private phenomenal experience (and since no one shares my private experience, no one else knows what the phenomenal sentences of my private language mean).

Indeed, since I can only understand supposed "sentences about external objects" insofar as they mean, or are logically equivalent to, such conjunctions of sentences about my private phenomenal experience, two points follow. First, such "external object sentences" cannot for me really mean, or logically imply, that there are external objects (that is, objects independent of my experience of them). My understanding of the meaning of any sentence is exhausted in knowing which sentences about my private experience would confirm that sentence and which would disconfirm it, and my understanding of the meaning of the words in these confirming and disconfirming sentences is exhausted by my knowledge of how these words (and the bits of experiencable data that they invoke) contribute to determining the truth conditions of these sentences.

Second, my knowledge of a certain kind of "external object"—namely, sentences of "public" languages such as English as they are written or spoken—must have the same status for me as any other "external object." My understanding of these objects and their meaning, or sentences about these objects and their meaning, is again wholly exhausted in my taking as confirming or disconfirming instances certain sentences in my personal phenomenal language. My understanding of, for example, "There is a bar of sulphur in the right-hand drawer of the dark mahogany desk in front of me" is twofold. I may recognize it directly as a sentence in my private language, as a type of phenomenal experience of sound (or visual pattern) that I associate with other verifying phenomenal experiences. (These are the conditionals containing phrases such as "impressions of muscular activity in my right arm" and "impression of a yellowish rectangular shape against a dark brown background," which were initially put in single quotes to reflect the supposition that these are purely phenomenal data which are not meant to suggest the existence of nonphenomenal objects such as arm muscles and

sulphur bars.) On the other hand, I may recognize the sentence as having that analysis and the additional role of serving in my solipsistic metaphors about an external world of objects such as minds, material objects, causal processes and so on. In its narrow and broad role however my understanding, and the only available understanding, of sentences and their meaning is wholly exhausted in phenomenal terms.

The reader may be puzzled that I should bring up classical and linguistic solipsism. Surely, it could be remarked, we need not consider solipsism as anything more than a curious epistemological byroad in the history of philosophy and psychology. While Hume maintained classical solipsism in the eighteenth century and we find linguistic solipsism in Bertrand Russell and in Wittgenstein's early work, one might suppose that it is now a dead position and in any case an extraordinarily eccentric one. However, I think that it is neither dead nor irrelevant, for as I shall show some current theories of meaning and language, and of individual knowledge of meaning and language, have retained linguistic solipsism, particularly in maintaining the phenomenalistic analysis of language.

Certainly, as I wrote on page 46, solipsism only has interest as the view that a private, phenomenal language is possible—a simple, extensional language whose grammar and semantics is wholly and uniquely accessible to the individual consciousness. Indeed, even an examination of classical solipsism such as that of Descartes' *Meditations* may be understood as an attempt to show that individual consciousness is irretrievably committed to "abstract" ideas—and specifically to the idea of substance or object permanence—that not only cannot derive from phenomenal experience but cannot be made sense of within the thought of a consciousness that employs a purely phenomenal language.

Wittgenstein's argument that a private, or phenomenal, language is impossible can be understood to run as follows. The form of argument is that of sketching what a private, or phenomenal, language would have to be like and then showing it could not be language, that it could not serve the minimal function of allowing its one speaker to describe that speaker's own experiences.

Suppose I have what strikes me as a new bit of sensual expe-

rience. I name it *grueson.* It could be some sort of ticklish twinge. But, of course, we are to imagine that there is no way for me to describe the sensation to anyone else. That is what is meant by our assumption that my language is in principle private, is a purely phenomenal language. I cannot in other words translate my sentence "*Grueson* here now" into a sentence that I know will mean the same to someone else that "*Grueson* here now" means to me.

Of course, from my viewpoint, I have not described something to myself in naming my new sensation "grueson." That is because my selection of "grueson" as the name of my new sensation is arbitrary. I could have called it "greenson," "bleen," "glory," "impenetrability," or anything whatever. So my choice of forging an association between a bit of my mental experience, namely "grueson," and another bit of my mental experience, my new sensation, is just a decision, not a description. By naming it "grueson" I have not told myself anything about it. I am here adopting what might be called Humpty-Dumpty linguistics:

> "I don't know what you mean by 'glory,'" Alice said. Humpty-Dumpty smiled contemptuously.
>
> "Of course you don't. I meant 'There's a nice knockdown argument for you!'"
>
> "But 'glory' doesn't mean 'a nice knockdown argument,'" Alice objected.
>
> "When I use a word," Humpty-Dumpty said, "it means just what I choose it to mean—neither more nor less."
>
> "The question is," said Alice, "whether you *can* make words mean so many different things."
>
> "The question is," said Humpty-Dumpty, "which is to be master—that's all."

Wittgenstein takes Alice's side of the question. He raises the issue of how we are to understand matters if the "new sensation" apparently recurs. Suppose I have another sensation. Suppose I say "Grueson here now" again. Is there any way whatsoever by which I can decide whether I have described the bit of sensation as "grueson" or chosen to extend the meaning of "grueson" to apply to this new bit of sensation? The crux of Wittgenstein's argument is that there is no way of deciding. I

cannot distinguish *naming* something or choosing a meaning for a word from *describing* something, that is, from deciding that a word in my private language correctly fits a new bit of my experience. Normally we distinguish naming from describing something in that we assume naming is in certain respects an arbitrary choice while describing is something about which one can be correct or mistaken. But the problem with this sort of case and with private phenomenal language in general is that it does not seem possible for me to be wrong, or know that I was wrong, about saying "Grueson here now," of this new bit of my experience. Hence I do not have a language even in the most minimal sense of a language that allows me to describe my own experience to myself.

There is of course an obvious response to this kind of argument. I might protest:

Surely I am able to tell whether this present bit of experience is the *same sort* of experience as the one I had previously labeled as "grueson." And if this present bit of experience is the same sort of experience that I labeled "grueson," then I will be describing it when I say to myself "Grueson here now" and if it is not the same sort, I will presumably be extending the meaning of "grueson" when I say that it is "grueson," for I *certainly* cannot be mistaken. (I might of course be mistaken in this way in speaking a nonphenomenal language. For example, if I have the name "gold" to a metal with a certain yellowish appearance which melted at a certain temperature, had a certain specific gravity, atomic structure, and so on, then obviously I could say that something was gold because of its appearance, etc., and be disappointed to find that it failed other, more crucial, tests.)

The response to my protest is to dispute the claim that *I am able to tell*, for my purely private, phenomenal language, what sorts or "natural kinds" of experiences there are for me, so that having labeled a particular instance of a sort of experience "grueson," I am able to tell for the purposes of my phenomenal language whether or not some subsequent bit of experience is another instance of this sort and so another instance of "gruesonness."

The problem with my protest, in other words, is that it

suggests that my mind makes use of some innate sense of sorts or natural kinds. It suggests that my mind will not take each bit of experience as wholly unique, and equally and wholly different from every other bit of experience. Rather, my mind will take each new experience as fitting into, as instancing, various categories. I will recognize new instances of "grueson" as being "grueson" because these new instances—while differing in accidental details—will have the same essential features, will fit the same categories. In other words, I will not simply make the association between my word "grueson" and my new sensation; I will not simply dub this sensation "grueson." Rather, I will recognize my bit of experience as a sort of experience and label this sort, any instance of this sort, "grueson." I will "know" how to go on, how to use the word to describe future instances.

Now it is indisputable that human minds do have tendencies to generalize in certain ways, to recognize particulars as instancing natural kinds, and so on. This is particularly evident in the way children learn and adults use language. Research in psycholinguistics makes it clear that the human child is extraordinarily adept at individuating speech sounds, words, and sentences as these recur in sound sequences of great variation and diversity. Similarly, adults continually and effortlessly individuate, in speaking and hearing, quite new sentences with complex structural features. But they cannot explain or even explicitly formulate their complex knowledge of human language. Though investigation shows that humans make use of extensive and detailed knowledge of phonology and syntax in individuating and understanding sentences such as "Flying planes can be dangerous," they are quite unable to formulate the knowledge that they have, unable to bring more than a small portion of it to a conscious level. Indeed, the professional linguist's own *conscious* knowledge of his or her native language is not acquired through self-analysis, through a penetration of the linguist's subconscious psyche, but through the examination of recurring features in various human languages and in language acquisition, and through abstract analysis of the underlying features of language that are presupposed by the ordinary speaker's conscious knowledge (recall Levi-Strauss' observation that "The transition from conscious to unconscious is associated with prog-

ress from the specific toward the general"). Similar remarks are in order respecting other aspects of hearing and sight. We are, for example, extraordinarily adept at recognizing human faces when we meet them again in unfamiliar circumstances and at unfamiliar angles, even picking out a face from a childhood group photograph though we have only known the adult. But we are not conscious of how we know how to do this.

But these regularities, these patterns of individuation and generalization, are not accessible to the individual consciousness. The individual consciousness cannot formulate, cannot know consciously, the rules that that consciousness may be following. Cognitive psychologists and linguists look to the *species* to discover, through examining the underlying tendencies of humans everywhere to individuate (or distinguish) and generalize experience, what must be true in the case of the individual mind. But this route, one which cognitive psychologists have only begun to investigate in real depth, is not available to the individual consciousness attempting to employ a private, phenomenal language. Supposing that I am attempting to speak a private, phenomenal "language," I may on occasion follow my species in recognizing a new bit of experience as another instance of a natural kind that I had named "grueson," while on another I may arbitrarily happen to extend the label "grueson" to an instance of another sort of experience. *However, there is no conscious way for me to know which I have done.* The distinction between recognizing another instance of "gruesonness" and choosing to enlarge the meaning of the word "grueson" is simply not available within my private phenomenal "language."

There is no personal, conscious solution to the problem of knowing a language or one's mind—just as there is no personal solution to the problem of knowing about the external world of material objects, minds, and causal processes. The classical or linguistic solipsist cannot section off a transparent and wholly accessible phenomenal world, that is, a world that the solipsist knows in describing it in a transparent and wholly accessible private phenomenal language. Rather, there is only a public language, that is, a language whose meanings, structure, rules, and items, as its attendant conceptual apparatus, is not at all

transparently and wholly available to the individual consciousness. I am in the world and I cannot talk myself out of it.

To recapitulate, I have a new bit of experience and "name" it "grueson." In my Humpty-Dumpty "language" what I have done is to draw a line of association between two unique bits of experience, namely, my new bit of experience and another bit of auditory experience, "grueson." Subsequently, I have another experience and wonder how I should describe it. Perhaps something like my auditory experience comes to mind, but there seems no way I can be sure whether this is the *same word* in my private language. Equally, and most basically, when I regard my new experience and try to decide whether it belongs to the same kind as, or can be described as the same as, the earlier experience that I labeled "grueson," I do not know what to say; that is, within my private phenomenal language there is nothing I can say that would mean anything to me. I may draw a line in my imagination between "grueson" and my new experience but I do not know how to tell whether (1) this line means to me that the new experience "is grueson" or (2) that I have chosen to expand the meaning of "grueson" to mean "is grueson" (in the old sense) or "is like my new experience."

A more abstract way of putting the argument against a private, phenomenal language might be this. To be in possession of a language—certainly any language with which one could describe the world—is to be in possession of a set of rules that generate an infinite set of sentences with structural descriptions and meanings (or semantic relationships). But an infinite set cannot be given by enumeration, so my belief that I, or anyone else, is in possession of a language is always underdetermined by any number of sentences or meanings, or rather tokens of such, that I or anyone else might exhibit. My belief that I, or anyone else, is in possession of a rule is never equivalent to any set of actual performances. For example, observing you to count "2, 4, 6, 8, 10, 12, . . . 98, 100," I may think that you are in possession of the rule for counting out the even numbers. But what if you continue ". . . 104, 108, 112, 116 . . ."? No matter how high you count I can always imagine you might go on differently. Similarly, no matter how many grammatical sentences of English someone produces, this production itself will never be equivalent to the

claim that that person is a competent speaker of English, or is in possession of its rules, for the person might go on to produce nongrammatical strings. (Of course, if the person *really* is in possession of English, and is properly motivated, it *is not* possible that the person should go on in that way, but it *is* possible of course *if* all we mean by saying that a person is in possession of English is that that person will produce some finite body of sentences.)

Why will the shift from a private to a public language matter? Well, it does matter in that one can then use the linguistic, and more generally cognitive, regularities in a number of different individuals (perhaps even regularities across languages) to narrow the acceptable answers to the question *what rules are they following?* much more than would be possible with *what rules is this individual following?*—but that is not the most important difference. For, as we shall see in the next chapter, it is inevitable when we attempt to describe a natural language that we take its speakers not simply to exhibit specified behavior but to be in possession (largely unconsciously) of an abstract grammar whose specification requires an explanatory theory of an innate language acquisition device common to our species. We require a level of linguistic description, if not more than one, that is not reducible to particular (conscious, phenomenal) experiences just as we need, and have, a language that makes *essential* reference to material objects, causal processes, and minds—that is, that uses sentences that cannot be understood as reducible to phenomenal conditionals.

Of course, the very way in which I had to explain linguistic solipsism suggests its flimsiness. Certainly this was apparent when I sketched the reduction of the material object sentence "There is a bar of sulphur in the dark mahogany desk in front of me" to the phenomenal language sentences "If I feel such and so 'impressions of muscular activity in my right arm and fingers' and feel such and so 'impressions of the sound of wood scraping on wood,' then I will have the 'impression of a yellowish rectangular shape against a dark brown background' in the lower portion of my visual field," "If the impression of a yellowish rectangular shape occupies an increasingly large portion of my visual field, I will have 'an impression of an acrid, breath-taking

odor,'" and so on. It is obvious that the simplest reduction of the material object sentence would be to sentences such as "If I open the drawer with my right hand I will see a bar of sulphur in the bottom of the drawer." But that, while much clearer than what I ended up with, still contains clear references to material objects. The reason I put the phrase "impressions of muscular activity in my right arm and fingers" in single quotes was to suggest that one means to refer to some *feeling* that one gets when one is moving one's arm and fingers but conceivably might get when one was not: the reference was to be to the feeling, to the "purely phenomenal" experience, without any reference to the real existence of public material objects such as arms and hands. Similarly, one was to refer to the "impression of the sound of wood scraping on wood" without supposing anything about the public, physical sound, or about wood, or about scraping as a physical process. Again one was not supposed to be talking about actual physical rectangles, sulphur, mahogany, physical effects on breathing, or the public existence of sulphur particles in the air. Rather, one is just referring to "phenomenal impressions" that one's mind perhaps might but need not associate with material objects and causal processes.

But it is obvious enough that the more I succeed in obscuring the reference to physical objects and causal processes, the more unclear the language becomes. And it is obvious enough that I have not really succeeded in eliminating such references. Considerations of this sort have led many empiricist philosophers in recent decades to concede that we must accept an "ontology of medium-sized physical objects," and that any language we employ in describing our world will require essential reference to material objects. However, as I intimated in suggesting that linguistic solipsism or phenomenalism is not really dead, it is not always clear what such philosophers have conceded, nor is it wholly clear that such philosophers have really conceded what needs to be conceded, that is, that the human mind has natural patterns of generalization that belong to the species and are not fully accessible to the individual consciousness (so that the individual's ability to use any language is intimately entangled in the real existence of the species and the world). What seems

to be given up ontologically may be taken back in the theory of meaning.

Further, it is not merely that one needs a nonphenomenal ontology of material objects. One also needs a nonphenomenal ontology of languages and minds, or, at a higher level of generalization, of language and mind, of mental faculties. A more systematic attack on the Humpty-Dumpty view of language, or, more positively, a demonstration of the nonphenomenal, universal structuralist character of human language competence and language learning, belongs to the next chapter. However, once we are talking of a real, nonphenomenal, humanly learnable, natural language—when our linguistics becomes scientific as opposed to speculative—it becomes possible to remark that of course a natural language could not have a single word whether "glory" or what have you that meant "There's a nice knockdown argument for you." Equally, respecting Humpty-Dumpty's further remark that "I mean by 'impenetrability' that we've had enough of that subject, and it would be just as well if you'd mention what you mean to do next as I suppose you don't mean to stop here for the rest of your life," we may go further than Alice's mild rejoinder, "That's a great deal to make one word mean." It seems simply impossible that there should be a human language in which a single word could mean all that, whatever Humpty-Dumpty or any other philosopher of language might choose to say. On the other hand, it is obvious that the phonological structure "grueson" could be a word of English or of many other human languages, that is, humans could learn to individuate it, to speak and recognize it, while other phonological structures could not be English words, and some sounds could not be words in any human language whatsoever.

(Of course, we could have an artificial code in which "impenetrability" "meant" all of that. Or, for that matter, a code in which "impenetrability" "meant" all of the words from the beginning to the end of Tolstoy's *War and Peace*. This nonnatural, or wholly stipulative, sense of meaning is clearly possible. But I have been speaking of *word* and *possible meaning* in the natural language context. In that context it does not seem possible that a human language should have a single word that means for speakers of the language "We've had enough of that

subject . . . rest of your life," just as in English "oculist" means "eye doctor." That is, it does not seem possible in a natural language that what is a word, a unitary grammatical and semantic item, should serve in the minds of speakers of the language as equivalent to a series of several sentences in that language.)

Wittgenstein concluded his discussion of the incoherence of an essentially private language by remarking in effect that our ability to possess a common natural language depends on certain regularities in the behavior of objects vis-à-vis our perceptual equipment, regularities that make objects such that they can be named and individuated by us. (Though Wittgenstein does not stress this, this applies, as I have suggested, most particularly to linguistic objects themselves—distinctive phonetic features, words, sentences, structures, meanings, and so on.) Equally, of course, this applies to our cognitive abilities in themselves. Our abilities in thinking, perceiving, and sharing aspects of such occurrences depend on underlying regularities in the human mind which are no more accessible in our immediate consciousness than the underlying physical properties of things.

Assuming we have had enough, for the moment, of the idea of a private, phenomenal approach to language, meaning, and mind, I will next consider public natural languages and empirical linguistics.

CHAPTER 3

Relative and Universal Structuralism in Linguistics

WITH notable exceptions most language study prior to this century was practical, fragmentary, and unsystematically descriptive. There was little concern with theories about natural language in general, about language learning and the cognitive psychology of mature language function, about linguistic universals in phonology, syntax, and semantics: in a word, little concern with *linguistics* as a scientific enterprise concerned with unearthing laws of human language and of human language acquisition and language function. The academic study of language, or philology, was literary, historical, and prescriptive, concerned with written texts, with authenticating authorship and historical period, with determining pronunciation, grammar, and meaning of texts in dead languages or outdated dialects. A more practical academic concern was with teaching classical Greek and Latin grammar and rhetoric; and a still more practical and elementary concern was with teaching school children to read and write their native language, though this had classical grammar and rhetoric as its source. On a still more practical or more prescriptive plain we had the production of dictionaries through which foreigners might acquire a working vocabulary in another language, novices grasp the specialized words of a profession or craft, or status climbers learn the diction of a more exalted or more excellent level. Indeed, quite apart from the lack of systematic, scientific study of language in general, there was little concern with the description of the actual realities of day-to-day speech in contemporary European languages.

This lack of concern with systematic, scientific linguistics, with the study of universal features of language and with the more basic aspects of contemporary languages, may seem strange

if we forget Levi-Strauss' dictum that "the transition from conscious to unconscious is associated with progress from the specific to the general." But there is a natural human tendency to denigrate common knowledge. If any normal human speaks and understands a (contemporary) human language at an early age without requiring or usually receiving any explicit instruction, it is natural that this knowledge is given little attention. Further, taking Levi-Strauss' dictum more seriously, the difficulty in acquiring a scientific knowledge of language and, in particular, of the first language we acquired as children, may be due to the fact that it is most difficult for us to notice and grasp consciously.

Consider as an example the ability to drive a car. When learning to drive a car one is highly and painfully conscious of all of the different things one must notice and of the complicated movements of hands and feet that one must undertake, particularly in shifting gears, steering, accelerating, and braking, and so on. But it seems essential that when one has fully learned to drive most of these actions do not take place at a conscious level. When one attempts to bring them to consciousness, as one might in attempting to teach someone how to drive, this is likely to produce confusion and a temporary decline in one's driving ability. Similarly, manuals for the somewhat more complicated activity of driving a motorcycle often insist that one will never drive well if one is conscious of what one does in shifting gears.

But surely this applies even more sharply to the activity of speaking (and understanding in hearing) a human language, for this is an activity that is intrinsically much more complicated, one that we undertake much earlier in life and one which is entangled in every aspect of our existence. It is obvious enough that not only is speaking and hearing one's native language an activity that is undertaken without conscious access to one's knowledge of the language but that the more basic and more abstract portions of this knowledge are not accessible at all to the individual consciousness. As a competent driver, I may concentrate on all I do in driving, and so eventually make these actions not simply accessible but present to my consciousness, with all the clumsiness that this would introduce. However,

I cannot, however much I try, bring much of my knowledge of English phonology and syntax into consciousness. In particular, I now believe that I do consciously know some of the phonology and syntax of English, and I came to this conscious knowledge through reading the arguments and data of grammarians and not through ruminating on my own speech and hearing, though I was a competent speaker-hearer of English long before such knowledge was present to my conscious mind. If, however, we consider myself at the age of six or seven, we find someone who spoke and understood English competently but who had practically no conscious notions whatsoever about English as a language. That is, I did not have the words "phoneme," "vowel," "consonant," "article," "adjective," "verb," "conjunction," "preposition," and so on, nor could I have been said to have any clear and conscious notion of the nature of language, words, sentences, grammatical rules, meaning, and speech sounds. Yet, in another way, I knew perfectly well what the quoted words meant.

For example, at that age I followed the rule of English phonology of using the *an* form of the indefinite article before words beginning with vowels and the *a* form before consonant-initial words. But I do not think that I consciously realized that there was such a rule of English, one that I had known unconsciously since the age of five or six, until sometime in my teens; and I was therefore able to formulate it consciously only because I had by then the explicit notion of "vowels" and "consonants" in my consciousness. Were I to try to consult this rule, among so many others, while speaking English, I would not speak the language fluently. Similarly and more substantially, my creation or understanding of new sentences at the age of six or seven revealed that I had tacit knowledge of English syntax, of the categories of noun, verb, adjective, preposition, and so on, and of the rules specifying possible structures involving words belonging to these categories, though I had little or no conscious knowledge of these categories or rules, and would have found speaking and hearing English an enormous burden had I to consciously employ these labeled categories and rules.

Again, when I first ran into Lewis Carroll's "Twas brillig and the slithy toves did gyre and gimble in the wabe. / All

mimsy were the borogoves and the mome raths outgrabe," I took them as English sentences, recognizing in the way I said them that "brillig," "slithy," "mimsy," and "mome" performed a role like other more familiar words ("adjectives," though in grasping this abstraction I had then no name for it). Similarly, I understood "toves," "raths," and "borogoves" to be plural forms of nouns and "gyre," "gimble," and "outgrabe" to be plural verb forms, though I did not have the English words with which to label these linguistic universals while speaking English. For that matter, though Lewis Carroll was doubtless aware of such matters when he wrote *Jabberwocky*, it is reasonable to suppose that he had no conscious knowledge of English phonology; yet like my invention, "grueson," all of his word creations are such that it is just historical accident that they are not English words ("gyre" in fact was an English word when Carroll wrote). His invented words conformed to his unconscious knowledge of English phonology. A similar example from recent linguistics is "Colorless green ideas sleep furiously." Though this sentence is perfectly senseless, speakers of English recognize that it conforms to English grammar and will read it aloud so as to suggest that they understand it to have the same structure as "Mindless Red bureaucrats rule rapaciously"; yet such ordinary English speakers may have little relevant conscious knowledge of English sentence structure, and no English speaker will make conscious use of this knowledge in giving "Colorless green ideas sleep furiously" the sort of reading that suggests that they do have this knowledge unconsciously.

Since nearly everything that humans think about, consciously or unconsciously, gets put into words, nearly anything can come up in the discussion of language. It is wholly natural that the linguist should try to circumscribe the subject matter of linguistics. Recent scientific linguistics begins in the attempt to isolate and characterize what belongs to language and to its systematic description, what belongs to the competent speaker-hearer of a language per se without introducing other competencies or characteristics. In particular, recent linguistics has taken the spoken and heard language as understood by ordinary native speakers as basic, while regarding the written and read language, and historical linguistics, as derivative. Rhetoric, logic, and literary

excellence are regarded as outside straightforward linguistics both in that linguistics is primarily concerned with characterizing sentences and their interior structure without considering larger structures such as speeches, arguments, and poems, but also in that the linguist is concerned with characterizing the ordinary competent speaker-hearer, not one who is extraordinarily, or necessarily, persuasive, logical, or aesthetically successful.

In a desire to insist on objectivity and to avoid confusing linguistics with other studies, modern linguistics whether relativistic or universalistic has taken a language to consist of a (presumably infinite) set of sentences with structural descriptions. To describe a language is to give such a set; to know a language is to know what belongs to the set. Phonology will describe the kinds of sounds and structural relations among sounds that delineate these sentences. At a more abstract level of structure, syntax (and lexicography) will describe the kinds of grammatical items, words and phrases, and so on, and the grammatical relationships among these items, so as to specify and structurally describe all and only the sentences of the language in question. Finally, semantics will specify sentence meanings and relations of meaning among sentences. (The status of semantics in scientific linguistics is somewhat in doubt, as we shall see. Some linguists maintain that semantics drifts outside of linguistics as a circumscribed discipline because it seems entangled in the rest of human knowledge and in other competencies. In any case, it is a much less settled area in linguistics than phonology or grammar.)

Notice that if we describe a language as a set of structurally described sentences, we will find it natural to say that someone knows a language, or has competence in it, if we can show in some way or another that that individual knows what sentences belong to the language and has some sense of the structure of these sentences. We might ascertain this if the individual utters numbers of sentences from the language, pronouncing them in a way such as to suggest appropriate knowledge of structure, and so on. But, equally, we could ascertain this if the individual, while listening to tapes of sentences of various languages and nonsentential noises, can distinguish which are the sentences of the language in question and show in various ways a grasp of

the structure of these sentences. Thus the definition of a language as a set of structurally described sentences suggests that the linguist does not think of speaking a language and hearing a language as two wholly different activities, each requiring a rather different sort of competency and knowledge. Rather, the linguist assumes that the same basic sort of knowledge or competence is involved in both speaking and hearing (along with some other, more differentiated abilities). That is why I have referred to the "speaker-hearer" of a language. Indeed, the two activities do seem to be mutually dependent.

Particularly in quite recent linguistics, the attempt to circumscribe purely linguistic knowledge, the conviction that the speaker-hearer comprises one subject rather than two distantly related processes, and the tendency to define a language as a set of structurally described sentences all lead to the belief that a "language faculty" is one separable component in a cognitive psychology, and, moving to a still more fundamental level of characterization, that a "language organ" is one separable component in human biology. For all the dubiousness of the historical regimentation that this generalization would imply, systematic linguistics has moved in the last fifty years from relativistic structuralism to universal structuralism.

That is, the first view of the linguist's essential task was that it consisted of compactly describing the peculiar units of sound and sequences found in a linguistic community over a time period (the linguist's corpus of data); and to this view was joined the assumption that the linguist or child language learner must learn these units and sequences essentially from the beginning, since no one supposed the presence of linguistic universals, that is, the existence of built-in features determining the way a human would generalize and individuate linguistic data. The whole language as the ongoing regularities implied by the finite corpus of actual speech may be imagined to take care of itself, at most requiring no more than the rudimentary powers of generalization available in all human reasoning and learning (suggesting, as in the analysis of the corpus, that there is no language faculty or organ in any substantial sense). The semantics of such a language perhaps would similarly amount to local and arbitrary associations between some grammatical units (word-sound se-

quences) and particular things, and between maximal grammatical structures (sentential-sound sequences) and situations in the local environment. (The Humpty-Dumpty, or relativistic-structuralist, notion of each language drawing its users into the prison of an arbitrary conceptual scheme comes in in that the arbitrariness of the vocabulary and sentential associations will equally suggest an arbitrary view of how the world breaks up into things and situations [facts, and so on].)

Next, and on the other hand, one has the now ascendant view that a human language consists of an infinite number of sentences with structural descriptions that can only be generated by (described or known by humans as) rules and abstractions of great power and depth. The corpus that the child language learner or linguist observes can only represent an infinitely small portion of the language. Moreover, much of the structure of these observed sentences exists only at a psychological level and thus can be "observed" in these sentences only by an individual who employs the same generalizations (has the same language faculty) as those who know the language. Hence, the universal structuralist assumes that the most basic task is that of determining the tendencies toward generalization and individuation of linguistic data that are innate to the normal member of the human species. (The contrast between relativistic and universal structuralism is more logical than historical, of course. Though the historical change is relatively clear cut in Anglo-American linguistics, Continental structural linguists were concerned with linguistic universals early in this century, echoing the Cartesian tradition of taking language as a mirror of the mind.)

The tendencies of the language faculty or, at the underlying biological level, of the language organ explain how the human child can learn the particular human language to which it is exposed (how the child in sharing a common human nature avoids the private language dilemma, though not at a conscious level). Equally, these tendencies underlie and explain the universality of various features of human language. This works both ways in that the universal lack of some kind of rule in human languages will suggest that the linguist should posit that the rule is unlearnable, that the child's language acquisition device cannot generalize in the appropriate way. Finally, the

universal structuralist supposes that whatever semantics we imagine for a human language must be responsive to human tendencies to generalize and individuate linguistic data as the human species does. For example, correlations may only be expected between what can be a *word* for a human and a thing (or kind of thing). Similarly, one cannot ask for correlations between some sort of situation and a sound sequence, but only between some sort of situation and a *possible sentence* in a human language—with all the psychological abstractions or underlying properties that "a sentence in a humanly learnable language" may have, as opposed to a physically recordable sequence of sounds.

But we can be more specific. Noam Chomsky, in *Syntactic Structures* (1957), implicitly began with a relativistic structuralist, or taxonomic, definition of language as a set of sentences that are structurally described (that is, with some specification of how this structure breaks up at various levels into clauses, phrases, words, morphemes, syllables, phonemes, phones, etc.). He then proceeded to show that on any reasonable understanding the relativistic structuralist (or taxonomist) cannot describe a natural language in anything like an adequate fashion. Equally, this showed that the relativistic structural linguist's notion of linguistic description and grammatical rule—of phone, phoneme, syllable, morpheme, word, phrase, clause, sentence, and so on—is in effect an empirical theory *and* a mistaken, insufficiently rich theory at that. This criticism then requires that we shift from the atomistic description of a (taped or transcribed) body of noise, a "grammar of lists" as in Zellig Harris' classic *Structural Linguistics* (1951)—"The preceding chapters have indicated a number of operations which can be carried out successively on the crude data of the flow of speech, yielding a compact statement of what utterances occur in the corpus" (p. 361)—to the formulation in *Syntactic Structures*, which makes linguistics essentially psychological: "Syntax is the study of principles and processes by which sentences are constructed in particular languages. Syntactic investigation of a given language has as its goal the construction of a grammar that can be viewed as a device of some sort for producing [generating] the sentences of the language under analysis" (p. 11). I stress psychological

particularly in that the native speaker-hearer of the language *is* such a device, and in that, given the radical indeterminancy of the full language and its grammar on the basis of a finite corpus (whether that of a linguist or the more ordinary language acquirer, the child), a wholly adequate description of a natural language requires the constraints provided by a general theory of natural language and natural language acquisition. The psychology is universal in character in that it is taken for granted that humans have a common language-acquiring capacity, or language faculty, and are equally suited to learning any human language.

It is incontrovertible that a natural language consists of an infinite number of sentences (if for no other reason than that the series of English sentences "I love the number two," "I love the number four," "I . . . six," and so on, obviously has no termination). That is why Chomsky claimed that "syntactic investigation has as its goal the construction of a grammar that can be viewed as a device of some sort for generating the sentences of the language under analysis," because an infinite body of sentences cannot be given by enumeration. In other words, the only way a human could know a natural language, or a linguist describe one, would be in having something equivalent to a finite, learnable set of rules that would generate the language.

A strict taxonomist such as Harris would limit the linguist to the physical description of the finite "crude data of the flow of speech" in a linguistic community during a given time. The relation between the finite described corpus and the admittedly infinite language is then conceived as one of ordinary probability. What distinguishes the sound sequences that *could* have belonged to the corpus (this would be the rest of the language) from other sound sequences is that the former are *more probable* than other sound sequences (such as sentences from other languages and nonlinguistic noise making). The simple response to this is to emphasize that since a language contains an infinite number of sentences, the probability of occurrence of an arbitrary sentence of the language is infinitely small. The probability that I will produce a noise sequence that will be recognized as some given sentence of English is exactly the same as the probability that

I will produce a noise sequence that will be recognized as some given sentence of Japanese—infinitely small (though of course I do not know the "principles and processes" by which Japanese sentences are created except the portion of these principles and processes that belong to all natural languages). It is for this reason that Chomsky rejects the very strict, or finitist, theory of linguistic description. But he speculated that the relativistic structural linguist's practice, as opposed to the strictest theorizing about this practice, in effect committed the relativistic structuralists to the view that a language could be described through the generative capacity of at most something like a context-free phrase structure grammar. Such a grammar would consist of phrase structure rules that would rewrite a single, nonterminal symbol as one or more symbols (for example, the initial rule, $S \rightarrow NP + VP$—the derivation, which creates a tree structure or, equivalently, a labeled bracketing of a sentence, terminates when all of the capitalized, nonterminal symbols are rewritten).

An interjection may help here. The rule, $S \rightarrow NP + VP$ is a phrase structure rule that says that a sentence may be generated by rewriting S(entence) as N(oun) P(hrase) plus V(erb) P(hrase). The sentence is by the same token "phrase structured" or label bracketed in that the final product, in which all capitalized nonterminal symbols are replaced by lowercase terminals or words in the particular language, will be structurally described as a sentence consisting of a noun phrase followed by a verb phrase. So, using the rules $S \rightarrow NP + VP$, $NP \rightarrow Art. + N$, $VP \rightarrow V + NP$, $Art. \rightarrow$ *the*, *a*, and so on, $N \rightarrow$ *woman*, *man*, and so on, $V \rightarrow$ *hit*, and so on, one might generate the following structurally described sentence:

$$\left[\left[[\text{the}]_{\underline{\text{Art}}}\ [\text{woman}]_{\underline{\text{N}}}\right]_{\underline{\text{NP}}}\ \left[[\text{hit}]_{\underline{\text{V}}}\ [\text{the}]_{\underline{\text{Art}}}\ [\text{man}]_{\underline{\text{N}}}\right]_{\text{VP}}\right]_{\text{S}}$$

When I remarked in speaking of Lewis Carroll's nonsense poem *Jabberwocky* that I knew the categories of the nonsense words in it while having no name for them at the age of six, what I

meant in effect was that I was in possession of a version of English in which I had the concepts of sentence, noun, verb, adjective, article, and so on, that is, I had a grammar with these nonterminals, but I did not have the English words "noun," "verb," "adjective," "article," and so on, nor could I consciously and explicitly express my abstract conceptual knowledge. All this suggests against empiricist and behaviorist psychology that humans may have conceptual knowledge which is not transparently phenomenal, not simple memories of past experience as one might remember a sound. An ordinary phrase structure rule rewrites a single nonterminal symbol as one or more symbols. But linguists now think that a human language also has more powerful *transformational* rules that take whole structured sequences of symbols and transform their positions respecting one another, possibly deleting some symbols. This would suggest that we have a much more abstract and nonphenomenal understanding of our language, one that implies that the child language learner must have a very structured, innate language acquisition faculty in order to come up with the grammar of the language to which the child is exposed.

Incidentally, $S \rightarrow NP + VP$ is a context-free rule in that it says that S may always be rewritten as $NP + VP$, whatever symbols surround it. On the other hand, the rule $S \rightarrow NP + VP / Z$, is a context-sensitive rule in that it says that S may be rewritten as $NP + VP$ *if* it is followed by Z. A full analysis of relativistic structuralist practice might suggest that they in effect employed context-sensitive as well as context-free phrase structure rules. The argument of the paragraph preceding this interjection and of the two paragraphs following it is simpler if one sticks to context-free rules but it does not depend on this.

In any case, the effect of this is that a loose relativistic structuralist grammar generates an infinite number of sentences that are structurally described through labeled bracketings at successively higher levels, each level up strictly consisting of just one or more items of the level below (ultimately reaching arbitrary sound units, so the vain hope ran, with higher level abstractions strictly defined in terms of the lowest level). A sentence, then, will be a string of phonemes with successively more inclusive bracketings indicating morphemes, words, phrases,

clauses, and finally the whole sentence, with a string of phonemes constituting a morpheme, a string of morphemes constituting a word, a string of words, a phrase, and so on much as a long string of propositions under conjunction might be successively concatenated at more and more inclusive levels.

But the trouble with even such a liberal taxonomy is that it cannot generate (all and only) the sentences of a natural language, nor assign them in many cases anything like a plausible structural description. Linguist's familiar examples such as "John is easy to please" and "John is eager to please" illustrate this latter point in that there is no way the relativistic structuralist can bracket these strings to make clear that the first has a transformational relationship with "It is easy to please John," while the language does not allow "It is eager to please John." Similarly, "Flying planes can be dangerous" has the kind of structural ambiguity that phrase structure bracketing cannot specify, that is, we can explain the ambiguity by supposing that the sentence can derive, via transformations that delete the parenthetical words and move the others around, from either "Planes (are) flying (and) (this) can be dangerous" or from "(One) (is) flying planes (and) (this) can be dangerous."

So the device which simulates the speaker-hearer's grasp of grammaticality has to be a variety of transformational device (or a variety of Turing machine, which is to say any rule-following device). The question was, and still is, *what variety of transformational device*?—since such devices are understood to have the power of generating literally any array that can be generated by rules (any recursively enumerable set of sentences). For, given no further restrictions on the power of grammatical rules, this would seem to suggest that human languages are unlearnable (this is a specific realization in scientific linguistics of the general problem raised by the argument against private languages).

This is, of course, the general point that Chomsky insisted upon in his critique of relativistic structural linguistics and in his defense of the view that humans have a very specific and constraining innate language acquisition faculty. Finite linguistic samples, whether those of the linguist or the child, leave human languages radically underdetermined unless one presumes general

constraints on the power of grammatical rules and the character of linguistic descriptions—these constraints, setting the limits on naturally learnable languages, would in effect specify the character of the child's language acquisition device. Without further restrictions on the power of transformational grammars than those given in the "standard theory" of *Aspects of the Theory of Syntax* (Chomsky, 1965), one can prove that a wholly arbitrary and highly unnatural grammar can weakly generate any possible human language (Peters and Ritchie, 1971, 1973; Peters, 1973). Peters and Ritchie's point is that there must be further restraints *or* the question as to what the grammar of a given human language is is wholly indeterminate and the language is unlearnable.

In other words, the linguist and the infant face the same problem. They are both exposed to some samples of a language and they wish to find the underlying *rules* that will generate, and so allow them to grasp, the language itself. If *any* kind of rule is allowed, then the problem is hopeless. There will be literally millions of very different answers to the question, "On the basis of this corpus, what are the rules that generate the rest of the language?"—*this* is what the linguist means by saying that the language will be *unlearnable*. But the linguist knows that the human child *will learn any* human language to which the child is exposed: essentially, the child will come up with *one* answer. Hence, the linguist assumes that the child has a severely restricted program for individuating and generalizing by rule. The linguist has to figure out what the child's learning program is, that is, what kinds of rules the child will adopt. Since the linguist does not know what the child's program is, the linguist tries to narrow down the kinds or power of grammatical rules allowed in describing human languages. The idea is that when the linguist has found the most limiting kinds of rules that will describe any human language, then one will have something like the program of the language learning faculty of the child. What Peters and Ritchie showed is that too much liberality in what is to count as a grammatical rule will allow various wildly improbable sets of rules to describe any human language. If the child could think in terms of such rules, it would not be able to learn a language because it would come

Type	Grammars	Automata	Languages
0	unrestricted transformation	Turing machines	recursively enumerable
1	universal grammar	human language faculty human brain language organ	humanly learnable
2	context-sensitive phrase structure	linear-bounded automata	context-sensitive languages
3	context-free phrase structure	push-down store automata	context-free languages
4	exclusively left or right branching phrase structure (finite state)	finite automata	regular languages

up with millions of different "solutions"—exposed to a lot of sentences, it could come up with "solutions" that would allow it to go on in countless ways, rather than, as human children in fact do, converging toward one human language.

I should add that while I will continue to talk of rules or languages being "learnable," this is itself something of an abstraction. Even the wildly unnatural rules that Peters and Ritchie mention are learnable in the sense that they can be followed out by adults, with many fumbles and mistakes, if they are motivated and given an explicit list of rules. And children find some of the actual rules of human languages learnable only at a later stage of learning and only with difficulty. Abstractly, linguists speak of "learnable" rules and languages, but the final goal would be a scale of learnability, some rules being learned early and with ease, others late and with difficulty, and some only with painfully explicit teaching. Equally, it is a fair abstraction to speak of someone learning a natural language as an infinite set of sentences or of a linguist describing such a language; but, speaking most strictly, all one can learn or describe is a system of rules because that is the only way a finite human being can have an infinite set.

Put abstractly, the problem transformational grammar faces can be put in terms of what may be called a "Chomsky hierarchy" of varieties of grammar, as in the table on p. 72 (partly derived from Bach, 1974, p. 198).

The question is how to fill in level 1 more fully: how to find a principled way of constraining the power of level 0 in such a way that we can fill out the notions of "human language," "universal grammar," and "humanly learnable language" (or, so to speak, "humanly recursive").

As E. Bach put it (1974):

It is apparent that the Universal Base Hypothesis [that is, that all human languages have the same phrase structure base rules and hence the same pretransformational deep structures] should be an empirical hypothesis that could be disconfirmed. What is wrong with the present theory is its extreme power. There are two possibilities: we must limit the power of transformations in linguistically reasonable ways, or we must enlarge the range of evidence beyond

that given by ordinary considerations of descriptive adequacy [through the psychology of language acquisition or explanatory adequacy]. (p. 265)

Of course Bach recognizes that these two possibilities could be expected to converge and supplement each other. The question as to what constraints there are on level 1, on generative rules, is an empirical one. That is why the answer requires linguistic and psychological research. Indeed, the generalization that human languages are (some variety of) transformational languages is an empirical generalization—a discovery that Chomsky made when he compared human languages and the linguist's actual practice in describing them with the impoverished theory maintained by the structural linguists—but it is the very crudest of generalizations.

A grammar in effect shows how complex structures are built up from a finite vocabulary and a finite set of rules; if the speaker-hearer has tacit knowledge of the complex structures, the sentences structurally described, we can conclude that the speaker-hearer knows the set of rules to the degree that we can narrow down the sorts of rules that could generate the complex structures. The problem of constraining the power of transformations so that grammatical descriptions are nonarbitrary (and languages learnable) can be put concretely; above all, it is the problem raised by deletions in grammatical derivations. Linguists propose, for example, that "Invisible God created the visible world" arises from "God is invisible," "The world is visible," and "God created the world," as one deep structure through several transformations which delete occurrences of *is*, *God*, *the*, *world*. The problem is to recover, from the surface sentence, the pretransformational deep structure, to find out whether, and if so how, the surface sentence is generated by the grammatical rules of English. Without constraints on transformations it is possible to establish, as Peters and Ritchie have, that strings can occur whose sentencehood cannot be determined recursively (that is, through any finite step procedure). In actual informal practice linguists rarely propose particular rules that have to lead to such results. The problem that has exercised Chomsky and other linguists in recent years is to propose general,

falsifiable, and psychologically principled constraints that will make grammatical descriptions as testable and revealing as possible (Chomsky, 1975).

But if it is true that Chomsky showed that the relatistic structural linguist cannot adequately describe the syntax of human languages taxonomically (as strings of phonemes, or discriminable noise-bundles peculiar to a community concatenated at successively more inclusive levels), it is also true that M. Halle and Chomsky, and other universal structuralist phonologists, have given good reasons to suppose that phonological description cannot operate taxonomically, or atomistically. There is no level in linguistic description where sentences can be individuated (discriminated and successively reidentified) simply as strings of phonemes, as recurring atoms of sound (Chomsky and Halle, 1968). Similarly, even deep syntactic structure has been shown to have its effects on the perceived structures of phonology (Bresnan, 1973). Such results dovetail with now commonplace evidence in experimental phonology that show that human beings often cannot recognize, nor discriminate, supposed phonemes, and that when supposedly distinct phonemes are lifted from sentence structures, they often prove indistinguishable as literal sound.

The upshot is that we cannot understand the human speaker-hearer to individuate sentences phonologically as strings of phonemes. Similarly, without understanding the human speaker to have internalized a powerful generative device we cannot understand the speaker to recognize wordhood or sentencehood (to identify, for example, "grueson" or "Flying planes can be dangerous" in a variety of accents and other variations in realization). The human speaker-hearer does not hear and individuate a sentence as a physical string of individuated sound bursts, and *then* individuate morphemes, words, phrases, and sentence as successively more inclusive concatenations. Rather, sound data, in itself insufficiently determinate, allows the competent speaker-hearer to recognize higher level pattern and structure that will allow the full individuation of the sentence. This is of course what one might expect, for it is basic to the psychology of pattern recognition that the manner in which a pattern is recognized and individuated depends on the perceiver's sense of the total set of possible patterns that might confront the perceiver

(that is, in this case the infinite totality of sentences with structural descriptions that constitute the speaker-hearer's language).

This upshot is particularly important for theories about meaning and translation respecting human languages that have been proposed by W. V. O. Quine and others. In *Word and Object* (1960), Quine suggests the following analysis of "radical translation," that is, translation in which the translator, who seems to be regarded as something of an anthropologist, has to learn the "native's" language from scratch. Quine more or less takes for granted the relativistic structuralist's view of the individuation of sentences, of phonology and syntax, and seeks to add a semantics to this sort of linguistics, which was still dominant when Quine wrote *Word and Object* though on the wane. Quine proposes that we must assume that the radical translator has no information about the native's psychology, the native's tendency to generalize and individuate in terms of the cultural bias built into the native's language. The translator can be understood to know everything about the physical features of the environment, know what physical stimuli (sound waves, "retinal irradiations," and so on) are hitting the native—but not how the native is taking them or internally representing them. Finally, the translator is allowed to issue sentences in the native's language and to expect an "assent" or "dissent" reaction from the native. For example, the linguist might say "gavagi" (a supposed sentence in the native's language) in a variety of environmental contexts, receiving a "yes" or "no" from the native. Eventually, the linguist might discover that the only prominent environmental feature common to all "assents" and lacking in all "dissents" is something the linguist might report in English as "Lo, a rabbit." The root idea is that one knows *all the semantics one can know* if one knows respecting each sentence of the language the situations in which the speaker-hearer marks the sentence as true or as false. Any question of meaning, of translation, that is left indeterminate by this remains so—that is, Quine's indeterminacy of translation thesis. For example, translation will leave indeterminate whether the native is referring to a substantial unity or "undetached rabbit parts," an instance of a natural kind or an accidental accumulation. (Since there would seem, equally, a similar problem for any speaker-hearer of English who takes

himself to be in Quine's situation, there would seem a similar indeterminacy within English or any other natural language.)

People sometimes wonder what the real point of the relativistic indeterminacy of translation thesis is.

Accepting that for a philosopher such as Quine both natural language(s) and the "language(s)" of science are both on the same footing, both theories about reality, one can understand the thesis as a claim that our knowledge (or even speculation) about the world and human psychology is limited to what can be expressed in extensional, first-order language. Further there seems a bias toward empiricism and phenomenalism in that mentalistic claims about underlying psychological realities are excluded from the determination of meaning; and the supposed difficulty in determining what the "native" means by "gavagi" may indeed suggest that even the traditional ontological notion of physical object or substance is excluded. More simply, in opting for extensional, first-order languages, through claiming that we can make no real sense of more powerful languages, Quine means to deny that we can have any meaningful sense of difference between accidental factual generalizations such as "All of the Earth's moons are airless," lawlike generalizations of physical necessity such as "Heat is the motion of molecular particles," lawlike biological generalizations such as "All cats are mammals," analytic truths such as "All oculists are eye-doctors," or even logical truths in the narrowest sense. In a way it is obvious that Quine would have to reach this conclusion, since he claims in effect that all we can ever know about the meaning of a sentence is that it has been marked true in certain situations and false in others; but since all of the generalizations of the previous sentence happen to be marked true, there is no available distinction among them for Quine in logical or semantic status. In a Quinean world all statements are on the same footing, and all have meaning only insofar as they are "couched in observational terms," insofar as they come down to "retinal irradiations" of certain sorts, "sound wave impacts" on ears of certain sorts, and so on.

In other words, the results of recent linguistics respecting the human speaker-hearer's individuation of sentences are particularly important for the empiricist philosopher's attempt to deter-

mine the semantics of a natural language up to supposed indeterminacy by having the "radical translator" produce its "sentences" in varieties of physical contexts and then waiting for an affirmative or negative from the native. The individuation of sentences, of structural identity, would seem to require that both native and translator share a sense of structural determinacy derived from a generative grammar that depends for its determinateness, and learnability, on species-specific tendencies to generalize linguistic data in highly constrained ways. In other words, one must grant that syntax, at least in the sense of specifying the relation of structural identity of expressions, the individuation of sentences, is logically more basic than semantics (that is, the relation of truth between a sentence and a context of utterance, and so on). As Hilary Putnam put it, "The relation of structural identity of expressions is more basic than the notions of semantics in two senses: the latter notions seem to presuppose the former notion; and the notion of structural identity is, I believe, not definable in terms of the semantical notions of truth [and synonymy]" (Putnam, 1974, p. 96). But then we find undermined the argument that translation is indeterminate if we move beyond truth (beyond Quine's austere first-order logic) toward more powerful notions such as analyticity, synonymy, possible sentence of English, necessary feature of natural language, and so on. It is undermined because it presumes that native and radical translator share an ability to individuate sentences that must itself be determinate much beyond the observable physical data available to the translator (or native when learning the particular human language to which the native is exposed).

Quine's radical indeterminacy of translation is really much more in order if the translator is nonhuman, an intelligent extraterrestrial such as one of our Siliconians of Chapter 1 with whom we would not share any tendencies to generalize beyond observable physical linguistic data in species-specific ways. Reflect on the enormous difficulties such a truly alien translator might have in individuating "Lo, a rabbit." The difficulty about individuating rabbits pales by comparison. That is, a truly radical translator—a member of a nonterrestrial and nonhuman species—would not be prone to individuate and generalize on the basis

of very degenerate and scanty data as we do. The Siliconian would not know how to go on, how to recognize wordhood and sentencehood and internalize a reasonably determinate sense of the syntax of the human language of exposure. For the Siliconian would be in a position of a strict Harrisian structural linguist. The Siliconian would have a corpus and no even faintly determinate notion of the infinite language from which the corpus is drawn, nor indeed even an adequate description of the corpus itself and its individuation from the human viewpoint.

The Siliconian surely might share with us a commitment to the truths of propositional logic and some suitably austere predicate logic. We might expect this of any thinking being, any being, as we put it in Chapter 1, possessing a language with an infinite number of sentences with which to describe the world, just as we might expect of that being a knowledge of arithmetic. We might even expect—and this would be supposing more than would be allowable with the Siliconian speaking strictly—that a somewhat more similar alien would in general be capable of seeing and hearing as we do. We might, for example, imagine an Alpha Centurian to be mammaloid and thus make use of a similar auditory and visual range. But we would not expect even the Alpha Centurian let alone the Siliconian to have the sensitivities and predilections that allow humans to recognize and individuate human faces, a localized and independent brain function of humans which can be eradicated through brain injury without affecting general visual perception. Even more, we would not expect true aliens to have the species-specific tendencies to individuate and generalize that allow humans to learn human languages and individuate general noise into words and sentences.

How, then, could the true alien learn to individuate human sentences and their structure? Since the noise leaves the language, structure, sentencehood, and wordhood radically indeterminate, the answer must lie in human psychology.

The alien would seek to find how humans individuate and generalize linguistic data. An acute alien would not be much concerned with how other terrestrial species (for example, rats, pigeons, and so on) would individuate and generalize linguistic data. Nor would the alien assume that different subvarieties

("races") would individuate and generalize differently, for the evidence that humans seem equally able to acquire any human language to which they are exposed (in their language acquisition period) would alone rule that out. The alien, after some research, might first discard the simplest and most testable assumption—namely, that the natives individuate sound bursts atomically (as objective sound without more abstract and distinctively linguistic structure) and that the grammar is regular phrase structure or finite state, that is, in effect an etching on the mental "blank tablet" of associations between nothing more abstract than memories of observed sound bundles and sequences of such bundles. Quite simply, the alien would reject the taxonomic or relativistic-structuralist view of what a human language is and of what a human has internalized in grasping a human language. In doing so the alien would reject the behaviorist or empiricist view of human psychology, at least respecting the language faculty—assuming of course that the behaviorist and empiricist view is empirical, one to which evidence has relevance rather than a verbal stipulation.

The alien might then go about its business in two convergent ways. First, it might amass an enormous amount of linguistic data, casting about for generative rules with which to individuate and generalize his data. It is hard to resist the supposition that the alien, whether Alpha Centurian or Siliconian, would take all human languages as dialects, as particular realizations of the "universal language" stock of substantive universals (abstract structural categories such as verb, noun, adjective, and so on, on which most syntactical rules operate), constraints on the form of grammatical rules, and phonological universals such as distinctive features. This would, of course, allow the alien to have some sense of *how* a particular dialect, a particular human language, *would go on* beyond the finite corpus the alien might audit, and it equally would help the alien to individuate and structurally describe particular sentences, words, phonemes, and so on, within the corpus itself (which might eventually make possible the Quinean "Lo, a rabbit—"yes"/"no" procedure).

Second, the alien might try to reconstruct what set of presuppositions about languages would allow a human child to arrive with similar celerity at the grammar of any human lan-

guage, to internalize on the basis of a small and somewhat degenerate corpus, the capacity for generating and structurally describing the infinite totality of the language of exposure. Granting it the benefits of present knowledge of physical anthropology, the alien might find its concern with the convergent descriptive and explanatory adequacy supported by the knowledge that humans have been using and evolving into language, and the physical lateralization of the brain associated with language function, for many hundreds of thousands if not several million years (Isaac, 1975). Since rapid and full acquisition of the human language to which the native is exposed must surely have considerable survival value (particularly in the long "prehistorical" period when language was humanity's only technology), the alien would expect evolution to have favored both humans with more exacting and powerful "anticipations" of experience and also languages (or dialects with local variations) which would lend themselves to fuller and more rapid exploitation by such anticipations (Lenneberg, 1967). Indeed, the alien translator might enrich its data historically. The development of language through history is often explained in terms of what is easy or difficult to learn, generalize, and distinguish, to hear and say, for humans. But, then, history is by the same token a guide to what belongs to our species' tendencies to individuate and generalize linguistic data (Kiparsky, 1972). (I will have more to say on history in linguistic explanation when we come to semantics directly.)

In sum, in an idealization of its search to individuate and generalize linguistic data properly, the alien would seek to determine what is universal to or essential within a human language, what is common and necessary to human language acquisition, what is inevitable and characteristic in the development and maturation of the language faculty in the species. The species is the route through which we may hope to secure, explicitly and consciously, the full individuation and generalization of the linguistic data we have respecting our own or another human language. As I suggested in the previous chapter, the *individual* human language learner may indeed have tacit or unconscious knowledge of that individual's own language, that is, this individual knew how to acquire any human language and

has acquired this particular one. But the only route for such an individual to acquire explicit, conscious knowledge is through a survey of actual human languages and the learning of them, from which one can explicitly derive the notions of *possible human language, possible human grammatical rule*, and knit these with the *necessary features of human language acquisition.* Thus Chomsky on occasion speaks of the form of grammatical rules as *a priori* for the species *and* as deriving from the biological necessities of the human "organ" of language, of linguistic individuation and generalization.

While one may say that the literal empiricist or relativistic structuralist account of language and language acquisition is seriously compromised by the universal structuralist or rationalist account of language learning—both in its highly abstract character and in its underdetermination by literal physical sound—one may wonder how to understand the logical character of the generalizations of transformational-generative linguistics. That these generalizations are modular is evident enough, just as is the transcendental character of the argument for universal grammar and the language acquisition device. My own view is that the most coherent line to take is that a generalization such as "Human language is transformational-generative" ought to be understood in the way that the logician S. Kripke proposes we understand a generalization such as "Heat is the motion of molecular particles"; namely, that it is a *discovery* of linguistic science, that it specifies what the scientific realist would regard as (part of) the essence of human language, and that the inevitability involved is not a product of various scientific conventions for description and measurement; that is, while it is a necessary generalization, it is not in Kripke's somewhat contentious sense *a priori.*

Kripke distinguishes, both in his specific semantics for modal logic and in his informal discussions of naming, necessity, and identity, between *a prioricity* and necessity (and, he supposes though does not argue, both are distinct from analyticity and, one imagines, tautology). He offers the statement that the standard meter bar in Paris is a meter long as an instance of an *a priori* truth (Kripke, 1972). Whatever one thinks of Kripke's particular examples—the logical apparatus and the view of

names can be fleshed out with quite different examples—what he wants to get at in distinguishing *a prioricity* and necessity seems to remain. That is, there are various scientific generalizations that we intuitively want to regard as having to be true while neither being so in the trivial and transparent way of "All oculists are eye doctors" nor in the sense of "provable in the language with which we describe our world," and among these generalizations some seem more a product of nature and others more a product of artifice.

A simple way to put my point is to say that a human obviously *could* be exposed to a (corpus of a) language, even one superficially and observationally similar to a human language, and find it unlearnable (or learnable only in a partial, incomplete, and nonnatural way). It is not that our minds or the operations of linguistic methodology would force any language phenomena (for example, in another possible world) onto the Procrustean bed of human perception and cognitive acquisition. *We could find out* that it was not a human language, just as we might find out, might discover, that we are wrong about our present generalizations about syntax (much as one can conceive of a possible world in which something that gave rise to sensory experiences indistinguishable from what we know as heat should turn out not to be the motion of molecular particles, nor of course what we designate rigidly by the term "heat"). Just as we want to understand "Heat is the motion of molecular particles" as a *discovery* about heat, so we will best understand "(Any possible) human language is transformational-generative" as a *discovery* about human languages. Thus Chomsky took structuralist notions of (possible) *language*, *sentence*, *word*, *phoneme*, and *grammatical rule* as in effect theories, and mistaken theories, about real things, and he regarded his own discoveries as discoveries about these same real things, not a change in subject matter, terminology, or methodology. Similarly, our alien could discover (indeed this is what my sketch supposes it to discover) what present-day linguistics seem to have discovered: that humans implicitly, and linguists explicitly, must employ notions of possibility and necessity in adequately individuating and generalizing linguistic data. The generalizations of this paragraph

would seem to hold even if one rejects my particular *de re* way of understanding what kind of modality is involved.

It is important to recall that Quine believes that we can attain a reasonable semantics through his "radical" translation procedure. That is, he believes that what remains indeterminate under this procedure—that which can only be expressed in a more powerful logic than his preferred extensional notation—is not essential. We can get along without it. It is enough, in Quine's view if we can correlate the native's acceptance of, for example, "Lo, a rabbit" with what is constant in a variety of physical contexts and missing when the native rejects the sentence, and so on with a series of other sentences (assuming, perhaps, that we share a minimal logic with the native). Indeed, so Quine would surely assume, we are really in the same situation with regard to our understanding of our own language's semantics.

The objection to this argument that I have put forward must be understood in its proper context. Quine's indeterminacy of translation thesis requires that native and translator are able to individuate sentences, to hold in common a notion of the structural identity of expressions. Upon examination this requirement can be met only if they share an ability to individuate and generalize linguistic data in a lawlike or essentializing way quite beyond the determinateness provided by the observed physical data. Consequently, Quine can only have the individuation of sentences that his procedure requires if native and translator are allowed a more powerful and determinate conceptual apparatus that Quine wants (indeed, the general sort of apparatus that Quine wants to show we can and have to do without). The dilemma, then, is this. If Quine sets aside the transformational-generative linguist's more powerful mode of description, the radical translator will not be able to individuate sentences and words (and so on). The radical translator will just be able to correlate individual tokens with particular acceptance and rejection contexts: the radical translator will not know when the radical translator is hearing the same sentence or the same word. The radical translator will not be limited to indeterminate (but for Quine acceptable) translation. There will be no translating at all. This is clearly unacceptable even for Quine. On the other hand, if we accept the transformational-generativist's

more powerful modes of description, then we have sanctioned—admittedly only with respect to the syntax of natural language—a form of determinateness (an employment of modal notions) that Quine's indeterminacy of translation thesis is supposed to show we can and do get along without.

Note that the argument I use has somewhat the same form as the argument against an essentially private, phenomenal language of the previous chapter. Indeed, the target may seem much the same. Quine has allowed that we must discard solipsism and begin with an "ontology of medium-sized physical objects," and he allows that the philosopher has no business subjecting science to a radical solipsist critique in the manner of the classical empiricists and logical empiricists. However, it would seem that Quine "takes it all back" in his theory of meaning and translation, for he here disallows an appeal to powerful tendencies of generalization and individuation of the language faculty shared by humans in determining wordhood and sentencehood (though as I have argued this leaves him with no beginning for his semantics). Equally, Quine's commitment to an extensional logic, the backbone of the indeterminacy thesis, rules out the kinds of logical discrimination required to make sense of the modular generalizations that the universal structuralist linguist needs to make about language and the human language faculty, about *possible* words, sentences, and rules, about *necessary* features of language and language acquisition.

Note also that I have not so far made any claims about the modal notions that disturb an empiricist, or relativistic structuralist—such as Quine most explicitly—namely, the semantic notions of analyticity, synonymy, and so on. This seems wholly proper not only in that the relation of structural identity between expressions is logically presupposed by semantics, by truth and synonymy, but also in that the central advances of recent linguistics have been in grammar narrowly speaking, that is, in syntax and phonology. In *Syntactic Structures* (1957), Chomsky took pains to set semantics outside the specification of grammatical competence, outside the linguist's narrow description of a language. The transformations of that work patently did not preserve meaning or truth—their purpose was to preserve

grammaticality or well-formedness, to generate all *and only* the structurally described sentences of the language—and Chomsky sketches reasons for supposing that the attempt to capture a complete semantic characterization of a language in its syntax would distort grammatical descriptions (Chomsky, 1957, pp. 92–105). In *Aspects of the Theory of Syntax* (1965)—what is called the "standard theory" by linguists though since emended in some respects by most—Chomsky does provide a place for semantics in the characterization of linguistic competence. But more recently Chomsky and others have returned to something like the skepticism of *Syntactic Structures* about meaning as part of a narrow specification of linguistic competence when this is distinguishable from the speaker's knowledge of the world. While many transformational-generative linguists take somewhat more liberal views about the relationship between syntax and semantics—for example, the "generative semanticists"—nearly all linguists today feel somewhat uncertain about how semantics figures in the specification of linguistic competence. A recapitulation of these developments casts some light on the notion of analyticity.

For linguists transformations preserve grammaticality, that is, if the input to the transformation is well-formed then the output will also be well-formed, and they function syntactically in generating and structurally describing the sentences of the language; that is, when we say, for example, that "Jack was hit by Jill" is a transformation of "Jill hit Jack," what we mean is that both sentences derive from roughly the same base or underlying phrase structure tree except that the passive form of the sentence went through an additional "passivizing" transformation. That this is the Chomskyan sense of transformation is particularly clear in *Syntactic Structures*, since there the phrase structure base generates simple *kernel* structures which are recursively manipulated by transformations—from the underlying base structure of "Jill hit Jack" we derive, optionally, "Did Jill hit Jack," "Who did Jill hit," "Jack was hit by Jill," "Jill did not hit Jack," and so on.

At the time that Chomsky was first publishing there was another sense of transformation available to linguists. Z. Harris used the term in an attempt—distributional discourse analysis—

to extend taxonomic methods to describe regularities in structures larger than sentences. Before he could subject paragraph, discourse, and so on, to such analysis he felt one should standardize sentences by, for example, changing all passive sentences to active sentences, the assumption being that this would not change meaning but merely stylistic nuance, thus expediting analysis. Transformations, in this Harrisian sense, indicate equivalence in meaning (paraphrase) *quite independently of syntax,* quite apart from, that is, the rules that specify grammaticality. Thus one would imagine that sentences that had no apparent syntactical relationship might be Harrisian transforms (paraphrases). For example, "Jill killed Jack" might be transformationally equivalent to "Jill caused Jack to be not alive," and "Invisible God created the visible world" might even be a transformational equivalent of the French sentence "Dieu invisible a creé le monde visible" (similarly for other human languages and perhaps Siliconian languages and so on). Thus whenever one finds two sentences to be equivalent in meaning for whatever reason, one will say that there is a Harrisian "transformational" relationship.

In *Syntactic Structures* Chomsky effectively pointed out that grammatical description should not enmesh itself in trying to specify such semantic or Harrisian transformations. He pointed out, for example, that while "Jill hit Jack" may indeed have both a syntactic (or generative) transformational relationship *and* a semantic or paraphrastic one with "Jack was hit by Jill," the second semantic relationship does not obtain between quantificational sentences such as "Everyone in this room knows at least two languages" and "At least two languages are known by everyone in this room," though they are as active and passive related by transformational rule in Chomsky's syntax. Similarly, Chomsky pointed out that while "John received a letter" might be a paraphrase of "Someone sent John a letter," there is no way to specify this in *syntax*—provided of course that we regard syntax as specifying how the formatives, or lexical items, of a particular human language may be combined. For a time, however, it came to seem that these problems could be in part overcome.

The "standard theory" of *Aspects of the Theory of Syntax*

provides a more ambitious and in various respects a more adequate, acute, and simpler theory of grammar, one which dominated transformational-generative linguistics for a few years before and after its actual publication in 1965. Recursiveness is provided in the base component by the rule that the category S (sentence) may be rewritten as S plus something else. Instead of having the base generate simple kernel structures that may be stitched together through optional transformations, the base component of *Aspects* creates a full deep structure tree with abstract "formatives" marking interrogative, imperative, and so on, which is manipulated by nonoptional transformations keyed by the deep structure markers. Thus "deep structure" is defined as the phrase structure tree with insertion of lexical items before the occurrence of any grammatical transformation. For a variety of technical syntactic reasons, this system worked better than that of *Syntactic Structures*.

But what also seemed to be the case—and the convenience of it seeming so had considerable effect—was that the syntactic deep structure now seemed to provide all of the information required for a semantic interpretation of a sentence *and* a more complete basis for interpretation than surface, or posttransformational, structure. Thus, for example, "Invisible God created the visible world" would have a deep structure tree that can be represented by the whole structure "God—God is invisible—created the world—world is invisible." Deletion in this case does not seem to lose us much, that is, there is one, easily recoverable, deep structure. But as we have seen in, for example, "Flying planes can be dangerous," deletion can generate a structurally ambiguous sentence, one deriving from two quite different deep structures. The more transformational rules are regarded as deleting from deep structures, the more the unclipped deep structures themselves are likely to be regarded as the key source for the semantic component.

In *Aspects* the semantic component becomes part of the grammar of linguistic competence, though its structure is still sketchy. What does come to the forc is what is often called the Katz-Postal hypothesis, namely, the general claim just mentioned that deep structure provides all the information needed for semantic interpretation, and the consequent specific claim

that grammatical transformations, phonological coloring, and so on do not change meaning. Those working under the assumptions of *Aspects* shared the theory that syntax could and should be specified quite independently of semantics. The claim was that in case after case a more careful but nonetheless purely syntactic analysis led to derivations in which transformations *happened to be* meaning preserving. But though this was the official theory, it is obvious in retrospect that the Katz-Postal hypothesis was in effect influencing the way syntactic rules were formulated. This influence is particularly apparent in the case of pronominalization and referential relationships (anaphora). Information such as identity of reference between nouns was introduced into *syntactic* derivations and pronouns were introduced transformationally as replacements for quite abstract deep structure elements.

In the mid-1960s linguists became more and more aware that the Katz-Postal hypothesis was not compatible with the Chomskyan syntactic apparatus. Although some purely syntactic analyses did make deep structure seem a source of semantic information, this simply was not always the case. Harking back to the quantificational example from *Syntactic Structures* of three paragraphs earlier, linguists pointed out innumerable cases where an apparent syntactic transformational relationship obviously did not preserve meaning. For example consider (1), (2), and (3), where the derived surface structure of (a) does not agree in meaning with the surface realization of its deep structure source; in (4) we have a typical case in which the simplest supposition is that the phonological component supplies semantic information (that is, stress on "and" makes [4b] differ in meaning from [4a]),

(1) a. Every woman votes for herself. *From*
b. Every woman voted for every woman.

(2) a. All pacifists who fight are inconsistent. *From*
b. All pacifists fight and all pacifists are inconsistent.

(3) a. Few books are read by many men. *From*
b. Many men read few books.

(4) a. Josef *and* Susan can't come to the party. *From*
b. Josef and Susan can't come to the party.

With the decline of the Katz-Postal hypothesis that syntactic transformations do not change meanings and that syntactic deep structures wholly determine meaning, transformational-generative linguists have disagreed as to the structure of the semantic component and its relation to syntax. But nearly all seem agreed that there is no one level of syntactic (or phonologic) structure that provides *the* information for semantic interpretation. Some of those who are labeled "generative semanticists" have been interested in tracing out as many Harrisian or semantic relationships between sentences as possible. At the most extravagant and metaphorical level this had led to the attractive but untestable claim that, for example, the same ultimate "structure" underlies both "Invisible God created the visible world" and "Dieu invisible a crée la monde visible"—generally, the hypothesis that all human languages have the same base component—and that, for example, "Jill killed Jack" is the realization in English of a "natural logic" formula consisting of two names plus a relational predicate compounded from the "atomic predicates of [human?] thought" CAUSE, TO BE, NOT, ALIVE (the capitalized items are not supposed to be English). The desire to amass informal data about semantic relationships or Harrisian "transformations" also led a few generative semanticists to some very strained grammatical analyses. It was proposed, for example, that the deep structure of a declarative like "The cat is on the mat" is really something like "I affirm to you that the cat is on the mat," and that (5) is ungrammatical, while (6) is not, because (so far as one can make out) (5) requires an anaphoric relationship between "I" and "myself" that a counterpart interpretation of modal logic rules out (Ross, 1970; Lakoff, 1972):

(5) Last night I dreamed that I was Brigitte Bardot and I kissed myself;

(6) Last night I dreamed that I was Brigitte Bardot and I kissed me.

By the end of the 1960s the Peters and Ritchie results among others led to greater emphasis on the need for general, principled restraints on the power of grammatical rules, particularly transformations. At the same time, it became obvious that *even*

a syntax with the (too unrestricted) power of *Aspects* could not capture the basis for semantic interpretation at any level of syntactic description, nor the possibility of having syntactic transformations map semantic equivalences. Whatever constraints prove the most adequate upon further investigation, it is clear that syntactic description can be expected to diverge even further from a neat mapping of our semantic sensitivities. Since many philosophers in this century have thought that philosophy "issues in definitions" and that all philosophical problems are problems about the semantic analysis of natural language, about what competent speakers of our language mean when they say thus and so, perhaps more should be said or repeated about this failure in the "subliming" of natural language.

To return to the argument on pages 43–45, consider two philosophical disagreements, one between an intuitionist and a classicist in mathematical logic, the other between a behaviorist and a mentalist respecting human psychology. We imagine both to speak in English and we are asking to what degree the linguist can help them through his characterization of English.

The intuitionist believes, for example, that a doubly negated sentence does *not* entail (have the semantic relation of implying) the sentence itself, while the classicist would accept this entailment. (It does not matter whether the intuitionist restricts the view to sentences about mathematical objects—certainly the intuitionist can put enough mathematical reasoning in English for the point to emerge.) Will the linguist's characterization of English decide between them?

I take it that it would be perfectly preposterous to propose that it can or should. One might take the line that the intuitionist and classicist are speaking different dialects of English, though this is an incoherent and absurd notion of dialect, one with the bizarre result that we apparently have to label the language of a Vietnamese intuitionist either a "Vietnamese dialect of intuitionese" or an "intuitionese dialect of Vietnamese," and so on, subsectioning the population indefinitely in terms of all the conceptual and theoretical disputes humans undertake. But even that seems unsatisfactory, because then they are not in disagreement. The intuitionist is giving a correct description of the way the intuitionist speaks English, and the classicist is also

giving a correct and different description of the way the classicist speaks English. I believe that the only plausible way for the linguist to act is to describe English in such a way that the description is neutral between intuitionism and classicism. Since one can also imagine disagreement, say, between prescriptivists and naturalists on the "grammatical form" of moral judgments, or between, say, nominalists and realists on the "meaning" of theoretical terms and so on, to be fairly far ranging, the neutrality principle would have a fairly broad application.

Similarly, one could imagine a behaviorist claiming that all English sentences that describe mental activity have synonymous counterparts in English sentences that merely describe human behavior, while a mentalist would deny this. Surely, this is not a question that is easily resolved by consulting the accurate linguist's description of English, or grammatical competence in English. Indeed, though many behaviorists would say that English sentences describing mental activity have synonymous counterparts (or suitable paraphrases) explicitly describing behavior, it is obviously perverse to interpret behaviorism as a claim about the English language. It is presumably best considered as a generalization about the character of the subject matter of psychology, not a comment on English language semantics. Since there are many behaviorists and mentalists who speak English, and since still more would join them in finding acceptable (or finding quite unacceptable) such supposed semantic equivalences, a prudent linguist would again strive for neutrality on the question in his description of English. That of course would be the general line taken by the prudent semanticist of English. Where unresolved theoretical questions seem to involve certain words or sentences of English, the linguist will either avoid characterizing these words and sentences in any relevant way, or in such a way that the case is unresolved—which would reflect the situation among speakers of the language. But if the question is resolved, if a discovery is made, then what?

In that case people will eventually speak somewhat differently. That is, some considerable time after the discovery was made that water is H_2O, people probably did begin to speak a little differently. For example, some might then find the sentence "It was water, and I wondered whether it was H_2O" to be

anomalous and the sentence "It was water and it was H_2O" to be redundant. But surely this would not mean that the linguist's characterization of English, of English language competence, should change. Whatever the prudent linguist's minimal and uncontentious characterization of such sentences, and of "Water is H_2O" itself of course, this characterization must seek neutrality, for exactly that neutrality is the best idealization of the standardly competent, and in no way specialized, general speaker-hearer of the language. Notice the importance of adjusting our understanding of the semantics of a language in terms of the history of the language. It is the way in which we came—through what we would call discovery and experiment—to regard "Water is H_2O" as obviously true and hence "It was water, and I wondered whether it was H_2O" as anomalous, the kind of historical account we would give of the change, that would mark "Water is H_2O" as a very different sort of sentence from "An oculist is an eye doctor."

Consider, as a further example, the generalization about cats that has interested H. Putnam, J. J. Katz, and others: "All cats are animals." Some maintain that the sentence is analytic, others that it is a straightforward contingent generalization like "All of our opponents are in jail," others that it is a necessary truth about what we have discovered to be essential to cats. Putnam, for example, supposes that we might find that the things we call cats are actually Martian robots, hence not animals, hence "All cats are animals" would turn out false and is not in general analytic (Putnam, 1962). Katz, on the other hand, suggests that it is an analytic sentence and that if cats should turn out to be Martian robots, all that would mean is that what we had called cats should have turned out not to be cats (Katz, 1975). Since the attitudes (in part, beliefs about the general character of science and of the realities to which science addresses itself) that lead philosophers to talk in different ways about such generalizations are fairly widespread and certainly persistent, the prudent linguist would hardly wish to describe the English language in such a way that these questions are fully resolved in favor of one or another such philosophical, or scientific, doctrine.

Similarly, and finally, the generalization that "All human

languages are transformational-generative" is itself subject to these strictures. I suggested some pages back that within presently developing linguistics this generalization might be best understood as a discovery, and as nonanalytic but (in some sense) necessary. But of course I did not maintain that this followed as a particular fact about the semantic interpretation assigned to a particular sentence by the linguist's description of English grammar or English language competence. I did not mean that any more than Chomsky meant, in his critique of the relativistic structural linguist's notion of "sentence," "language," "word," "phrase," "grammatical rule," and "phoneme," that they were wrong about how these words are used in English, wrong about a very restricted part of English language semantic competence. They were wrong about what these words designate, wrong about language, words, phrases, grammatical rules, and phonemes, not about the English words "language," "word," "phrase," "grammatical rule," and "phoneme."

The moral is that the linguist's attempt to map some Harrisian semantic equivalences and to produce some minimal and uncontentious characterization of English language semantics does not, and should not purport to, solve serious theoretical questions of philosophy, logic, and science. And the moral has this example behind it. During much of the 1960s, an attempt was made to shape grammatical description to serve just such an end, and this had the effect of producing doubtful judgments of grammaticality, extraordinarily question-begging analyses, and untestable though alluring speculations about the universal base and atomic semantic predicates. With the realization that semantic interpretation requires inputs from several portions of syntactic and phonological description and doubtless depends on factual information and a variety of considerations, came also the general realization that syntax needs more restrictions on the form of transformations, and further provision for a convergence between the problem of the learnability of language and the testability of grammatical analyses.

In sum, we need neither to "sublime" the linguist's description of natural language, or of the normal speaker-hearer's linguistic competence, into a fabric which contains rich solutions to conceptual and theoretical problems, nor denude it into an austere

notion that excludes such solutions as senseless. Both views suggest an unwillingness to accept ordinary language as a vehicle within which deep conceptual disagreements take place; both attempt to embed solutions to general philosophical and scientific issues in the linguist's characterization of a natural language; both are unwilling to understand linguistics as an empirical discipline; and both fail to see that linguistics as a science depends on isolating linguistic competence and what belongs to the linguistic faculty from general conceptual problems.

My argument against requiring linguistics to provide a fully realized semantics can be put very simply. What I am defending is the view that there is a discrete language faculty—that it is possible, indeed salutary, to discriminate language and so linguistics from other cognitive faculties, and from conceptual and theoretical truth. By taking various conceptual and theoretical issues and asking how the prudent linguist would characterize sentences which the sides in these disputes would understand quite differently, I show the need for neutrality, the need to say that such disputes are communicated within natural language, not solved in the linguist's characterization of them. I am returning to the whole basis for considering linguistics a legitimate science, namely, that it is possible to characterize linguistic competence without finding every other competence, every other faculty, every other conceptual truth, delineated within it.

While universal structuralism eschews relativistic structuralist, or Humpty-Dumpty, linguistics and calls for a mentalistic psychology, it must resist subliming, must preserve the modular separation of competencies that is basic to a psychology of cognitive faculties. It must resist the seductive attempt to cram all psychological truth if not all theoretical truth into one system, into language. It must resist Roland Barthes' claim that there is

> . . . one final proposition that justifies all semio-critical research. We see culture more and more as a general system of symbols, governed by the same operations. There is unity in this symbolic field: culture, in all its aspects, is a language. Therefore it is possible today to anticipate the creation of a single, unified science of culture. . . .

Discourse is not simply an adding together of sentences: it is, itself, one great sentence. (in De George, p. 157)

Or again, it must resist Umberto Eco's claim that

The whole of culture must be studied as one phenomenon of communication. Semiotics covers the whole field of culture (or social life). The whole of social life can be viewed as a sign process, or as a system of semiotic systems . . . of *zoosemiotics*, the study of *olfactory and tactile communication, culinary codes, medical semiotics* (becoming a branch of a general semiotics), *musical codes, formalized languages, secret alphabets, grammatology* (as the study of writing), *visual communications* in general(*graphic systems, iconic signs, iconography* and *iconology, card games, riddles, divination systems, systems of objects and architectural forms, plot structures, kinship structures, etiquette systems, rituals, the typology of cultures,* and so on, as far as the upper levels of *rhetorical systems* and *stylistic devices.* (in Robey, p. 61)

In principle, the case against such extravagances is just that linguistics is a separable discipline, and linguistic competence is a separable faculty. The powerful arguments that have made universal structuralist linguistics a key justification for a mentalist or rationalist psychology and which show the inadequacy of behaviorist or empiricist psychology, depend on the possibility of this separation. Historically, the case is that we can make better sense of language change and of differences in language use that subdivide users into nonlinguistic, nondialectical professions, drafts, hobbies, philosophies, social interests, and so on, if we hew to the principle of linguistic neutrality.

Let me add one final word in favor of a very traditional view about philosophy. It is a commonplace that linguistics can be thought to contribute to philosophical inquiry (and psychological theory) in two rather different ways. One might hope that linguistics (and psycholinguistics) could provide very general information about natural language, human language acquisition, and linguistic competence. On the other hand, one could hope that linguistics might assist armchair philosophers who see linguistic analysis as central to philosophy with more scientific semantic and syntactic characterizations of specific sentences

(words, propositions, speech acts, and so on). An instance of the first route that we have been considering would be the claim that recent work in linguistics calls into question some empiricist and behaviorist views about how we learn a natural language, and about the logical character of the knowledge that we have when we have learned a natural language. Insofar as we regard the parallel empiricist and behaviorist account as itself deriving from a perspicuous overview of the empirical theories of psychology and linguistics, as Quine's radical translation argument suggests, we may also find this view an instance of the first route (Quine, 1972, pp. 1–3).

An instance of the second route would be the attempt to use recent work in linguistics as a tool in understanding causality and related notions through the analysis of sentences in which appear words such as "cause," "effect," "belief," "knowledge," and so on (Vendler, 1967, 1972). Another example of this second route might be the claim that recent scientific linguistics shows us how to identify and assign the proper logical analysis to the analytic sentences that some philosophers have thought were the basic avenue for all genuine philosophical inquiry. The second route was exemplified even before the advent of transformational-generative linguistics by J. L. Austin's attempt to solve philosophical problems by bringing to bear, on various doings and sayings with philosophically intriguing words, specialized knowledge of language that would take its place, as bits and pieces, in the scientific linguist's full syntactical, semantical, and pragmatical characterization of English (Austin, 1962).

One might label the first route *theoretical* and the second *practical*. Apart from convenience in reference, this labeling emphasizes that the theoretical route takes it that linguistics *and philosophy* are theoretical disciplines and that linguistics makes its contribution to philosophy at its most universal levels of generalization (and not of course through characterizations of a small number of English words or sentences). The practical route, on the other hand, is often put forward by those who hold philosophy to be a practical discipline (whether that of "linguistic therapist" or "journeyman logician"), one that the linguist may assist through the provision of plain facts, and very low level generalizations, about certain words and sentences.

Here I want to add that the theoretical route has much to be said for it whether or not this work continues to support a universal structuralist view of human language, while the practical route has proved dubious both in principle and in specific instances. I have tried to suggest that the recent history of transformational-generative linguistics bears out this point, particularly since the attempt to shape linguistic description so that it aptly served the practical route led to mistaken and now somewhat discarded views within linguistics. The argument that linguists must maintain neutrality in giving the semantics of the many sentences that are subject to contentious philosophical construals is an attempt on my part to raise an objection in principle to the practical route. The view I try to justify respecting linguistics and philosophy is one which has generally done well when considering the relationship between other sciences and philosophy—indeed, in the next chapter I shall try to show that some other human sciences can make similar contributions.

The more general and theoretical portions of the work of Einstein, Heisenberg, and others in physics have led to revisions in philosophy and philosophy of science. Similarly, philosophers have been concerned with the most general results, and theoretical implications, of the work in logic and mathematics of Frege and Cantor and more recently of Kurt Gödel. And, if Quine is right in saying that gestalt psychologists have shown the inadequacy of traditional empiricism and methodological skepticism, this might also be a case in which scientific work at its most general and theoretical level impinges upon philosophy (Quine, 1972, pp. 1–3). On the other hand, one may now feel less enthusiasm respecting those who have found proper philosophy to consist of stern therapy for the contradictory and incoherent through the marshalling of "plain facts" about the philosopher's unconscious psyche, class perspective, or ethnic sensitivities. One does not, of course, deny that philosophers have psyches, class perspectives, or ethnic sensitivities. One only denies that the provision of such facts, and the unmasking that goes with them, should be the primary or only legitimate form of philosophizing. Rather, such supposed diagnostic facts come in only after the primary task of showing the philosopher's theory to be false or empty has been achieved or granted—as

such facts might be used to explain various denunciations of the theory of evolution in this century, or die-hard defenses of the genetic theories of Lysenko or Shockley. Truth first, denunciation afterward, is the logical order of the day.

CHAPTER 4

Universal Structuralism Outside Linguistics

ROLAND Barthes defines (relativistic) structuralism as a method for the study of cultural artifacts, or signs, which originates in the methods of contemporary (relativistic) linguistics (Barthes, 1967). But there is not in any striking or useful sense a general science of signs (apart from mathematics, including mathematical logic, itself) just as there is no general science of "organized things" (apart from biology, chemistry, and physics, and of course mathematics). Perhaps anything that we would call a language (anything we would call thinking or even real) would conform to some very basic and weak logic. But this would not only tell us what was common to all our "sign systems," all our faculties and actions, but also what was common to that as well as to the signing and thinking of Siliconians, Alpha Centurians, and so on. But that would tell us very little. To the degree that there can be powerful and deep human sciences on the level with linguistics, they will be *human* sciences, taking faculties natural and innate to humans as their bases. There will not be, nor can there be, sciences of culture in general (that is, including Siliconians, Alpha Centurians, wolves, and so on), socialization in general, learning in general, economic activity in general, seeing in general, artifacting in general, "face to face" interactions in general, eating in general, food preparation in general, sexual activity in general, and so on, though there may be significant human, or natural human, sciences of some of these.

Similarly, we must resist the claim that "the methods of linguistics and the social sciences are different from those of the natural sciences," which Jonathan Culler seconds in ascribing it to Trubetzkoy:

Whereas the phonetician is concerned with the properties of actual speech-sounds, the phonologist is interested in the differential features which are functional in a particular language, the relations between sounds which enable speakers of a language to distinguish between words. It is clear that these tasks cannot be accomplished by the methods of the natural sciences, which are concerned with the intrinsic properties of phenomena themselves and not with the differential features which are bearers of social significance. In other words, in the natural sciences there is nothing corresponding to the distinction between *langue* and *parole*: there is no institution or system to be studied. The social sciences, on the other hand, are concerned with the social use of material objects and must therefore distinguish between the objects themselves and the system of distinctive or differential features which give them meaning and value. Attempts to describe such systems, Trubetzkoy argues, are closely analogous to work in phonology. The example he cites is the ethnological study of clothing. Many features of particular physical garments which would be of considerable importance to the wearer are of no interest to the ethnologist, who is concerned only with those features that carry a social significance. Length of skirts might be an important differential feature in the fashion-system of a culture, while the materials from which they were made were not. The ethnologist tries to reconstruct the system of relations and distinctions which members of that society have assimilated and which they display in taking certain garments as indicating a particular life-style or social condition. He is interested in those relations by which garments are made into signs. (Culler in Robey, 1973, p. 23)

But recent work in linguistics, indeed in phonology itself, suggests that while of course the linguist is interested in the "differential features which are functional in a particular language," the linguist strives for a general theory of human language and language acquisition, one which places heavy and natural constraints on what "differential features" could occur, and indeed is the only sort of theory which makes possible principled identification and description of these "differential features." The universal structuralist might rather suggest that "differential factors" in linguistics would be comparable, for example, to local cultural factors in the study of visual perception.

Doubtless local cultural factors do affect the way we see—as do individual experience and endowment, particular skills, oc-

cupations, and so on. For example, psychological experiment appears to show that the ability of North Americans to recognize words briefly flashed on a screen is "differentially affected" by even mildly taboo words—insult or curse words, words with embarrassing sexual or excremental functions. Cancelling out other factors such as complexity and obscurity and so on, mildly taboo words require considerably longer exposure for definite identification. However, it is reasonable to conclude that there is unconscious recognition—specifically since extreme brief exposure to taboo words causes measurable nervous reactions (sweating, change in blood pressure, and so on) long before conscious recognition occurs, and since a pattern of wild misguesses only occurs respecting taboo words (for example, not the ordinary misguessing of "band" for "bank" but rather of "curl" for "bitch," and so forth). All this is quite interesting.

But a moment's reflection makes one realize that this "differential feature" is an insignificant and superficial matter in terms of a theory of the human visual faculty and, still more important, that one can make coherent sense of this "differential" information itself only within the context of such a universal psychological and physiological theory. That is, when we try to imagine the system of visual processing involved, we must first suppose that the subject's visual program shifts into some specialized system for recognizing letters and words. (The existence of specific letter recognition malfunction—dislexia—suggests that something more specialized than general visual ability is at work; equally, the evidence pointing to genetic factors at least suggests that "differential factors" are not very important—no one speaks of "German dislexia" or "English dislexia," though it does seem possible that differences between Roman and Arabic letters might be significant.) Only at some late point in this process will words be recognized sufficiently for a censoring process to abort the full intrusion of the word into conscious thought. One presumes that a similar censorship process occurs respecting hearing and, perhaps, less specifically linguistic visual processing. Generally it is hard to make sense of the notion of "differential" cultural influences on these sorts of perception without supposing them to operate upon the essentially complete outputs of other, more fundamental and more universal functions.

In the first analysis linguists treat questions of the "propriety" of certain words and sentences as extralinguistic, as outside the narrow specification of the language faculty, simply because they do not see the division of a linguistic community into the prim and the nonprim as dialectual, that is, as correlative with a number of other linguistic distinctions in the manner of genuine dialects and as *not* correlative with a number of obviously nonlinguistic uniformities. On the contrary, the prim are presumably indiscriminatively proper in word, thought, and deed, and in different languages. But in the final analysis linguists treat questions of "propriety" as outside linguistic competence, because they assume that the best picture of our psychology is one in which the linguistic faculty operates separately from some sexual and excremental censorship process which acts upon the outputs of the linguistic faculty, visual perception and hearing generally, and presumably on outputs of other cognitive faculties.

Similarly, studies of "differential factors" in a culture in which racial distinctions are emphasized seem to show that an American white on brief exposure to a drawing will "see" the knife held by a white fighting a black in the black's hand. And one has evidence of similar displacement under other perceptual functions. But one can only understand this as a later learned censor function operating on an underlying innate faculty—the knife is seen naturally and then displaced by the intervention of a culturally induced override. When examined closely the actual factors involved in the seeing of various animal species are extraordinarily different, some responding only to motions in particular directions, others only to certain shapes and patterns—almost as if each species is programmed to read nature only in its unique way. Of course, individual members of these species learn something of local "differential" conditions into which they are born but only within the innate structure of their special program. And we can make sense of the learning process only if we conceive of it as the interaction of unusual local factors, environmental "differentials," within the innate faculty program. Gestalt psychologists are particularly concerned with "ambiguous" objects such as drawings that can be seen as a rabbit or a duck, as a face or a goblet, or "distorted" rooms

which are seen very differently once the subject has been allowed to walk into them. The point of this concern is to bring out the structured character of the innate program, to show where actual experience may push it one way or another, to show the underlying principles employed by humans in visual perception. The fact that a drawing may be seen as a face or a goblet shows what is happening in nonambiguous cases just as the fact the "Flying planes can be dangerous" may be heard in two very different ways shows that other sentences have a deeper structure than we might otherwise be likely to look for.

Again, it is a familiar fact that humans tend to find that humans of other ethnic groups "all look alike." Our extraordinary facial recognition faculty, which is separable both physiologically and psychologically from general visual perception, clearly develops on exposure to humans and will so develop respecting whatever varieties of human faces to which one is exposed. "Differential" racist cultural factors or simple lack of exposure—perhaps these come to the same—will suppress this extraordinary faculty. But it is not as if anything very complicated is learned in "learning" *not* to recognize and individuate faces of a proscribed group; and it is quite impossible not to assume that all normal humans start out with the same capacity, the same abstract program, and that they then mature recognition abilities along the same lines whatever the kinds of human faces to which they are exposed. It is a self-serving prejudice to think that humans alone among animals lack rich, species-specific innate programs for visual perception.

Of course, it is easy enough to understand the human illusion that we all really see the world the way it really is—the way a camera or "unbiased observer of any species" would see it—while thinking that "cultural differentials" in seeing are the only factors of genuine interest. Indeed, it is another illustration of Levi-Strauss' thesis that "transition from conscious to unconscious is associated with transition from the particular to the general." Similarly, as I noted, the study of language was initially a study of exceptional literary grace and rhetorical impact, of the language or accent of the learned or exalted. Simple competence in a vernacular, spoken language seemed so natural and commonplace as to escape notice, and with it

any real attempt to specify the universal and formal features underlying this ordinary competence—though recent scientific linguists reverse this order, since simple competence in a particular language can only be specified assuming a general theory of language acquisition and of linguistic universals, and literary grace and rhetorical impact as learned flourish—or private school accent—can only be described against the fundamental theory of plain competence. Indeed, the view that we "see the world as it really is" apart from some "differentials" of arbitrary local culture is of a par with the claim of the Enlightenment French philosopher Diderot that French is the natural language of thought (as opposed, for example, to English which is suitable to colorful rhetoric, and so on).

Again, relativistic structuralists have tried to suggest that each human culture splits up the visual spectrum quite differently in accord with "differential features" of each such system of social institutions—as is suggested, for example, by the fact that French has no precise equivalent for what Anglo-Americans call brown or by the fact that some languages only have three or four color words. But more recent research in "differential features" in color perception seems rather to show that humans in fact distinguish eleven basic colors—in particular, in order of dispensability, black, white, red, green, yellow, blue, brown, and, in no definite order, purple, pink, orange, and grey (Berlin and Kay, 1969). Cultures that have words for only two colors will have black and white, with three, black, white, and red, with four, black, white, red, and green, and so on up to brown (which seems to come in when a culture meets up with industrial manufacture or its products). In other words, it would seem that humans are conceptually equipped with eleven color categories in an order of relative centrality and dependence in visual perception (which probably is mirrored in the order in which color concepts are fully recognized or vocabulary learned by the child). All that the "differential features" of particular cultures determine is a selection, with some choice on borderlines, of how many of the eleven colors will be available from this innately differentiated spectrum in the particular culture's thought or, at least, vocabulary. Even this choice is limited by the universal ordering from black to brown sketched above. Thus

one sees again that it is not that each culture, in an arbitrary and complex manner, slices up and structures what its members perceive through a "system of distinctive and differential features which give them meaning and value." Rather each culture makes a very constrained set of choices within a universal, richly and deeply structured system of distinctions that the human organism is naturally, not socially, heir to in its normal maturation.

Similarly, while empiricist philosophers and relativistic structuralist psychologists such as Jean Piaget and W. V. O. Quine have suggested that the human infant begins life needing the "differential" input of the local environment to develop the idea of substance or "object permanence," more recent experiment seems to show that the human infant has this idea innately (Bower, 1971). (While the faculties underlying visual and auditory perception have so far provided the richest and most clear examples of cognitive universals, there seems good reason to think, for example, that Levi-Strauss is right in pursuing universals in such age-old human activities as eating and food preparation, in dress and deportment, in aspects of socialization and kinship and family formation.)

There are three fundamental problems with the relativistic structuralist view that Culler applauds in Trubetzkoy:

> It is clear that these tasks cannot be accomplished by the methods of the natural sciences, which are concerned with the intrinsic properties of phenomena themselves and not with the differential features which are bearers of social significance. In other words, in the natural sciences there is nothing corresponding to the distinction between *langue* and *parole* [between a language and the individual speech activities of its users]: there is no institution or system to be studied. The social sciences, on the other hand, are concerned with the social use of material objects and must therefore distinguish between the objects themselves and the system of distinctive or differential features which give them meaning and value.

First, this analysis makes biology impossible (or not a natural science). Second, this analysis, particularly of natural science, can only be understood as nothing more than a very contentious (and I think obviously misguided) denial of scientific realism. Third, this analysis is simply false as I have suggested.

First, if we change the penultimate word in the first quoted sentence from "social" to "biological," we suggest more explicitly that biology cannot be a natural science, for what is more central to biology than to understand the environment surrounding organisms as structured in terms of the differential biological significance of aspects of this environment for such organisms. To go to the microcenter of biology, the living cell of course has such a differential relationship to its surroundings. It is variably permeable to some surrounding chemicals, impermeable to others, some nourishing the cell, others disorganizing it. Thus the cell could be understood to imply one sort of value for salt in the environment, another for water, another for citric acid, and so on; and one could take the essential structure of the cell (at whatever level of generality one selects) and what it implies in relation to the environment to constitute a system (*langue*), while distinguishing this from the peculiarities of individual cells (*parole*). To go to the macrocenter, the whole of the biochemical physical environment of Earth is the subject of an ecology which, in its most comprehensive sense, must be understood as a system of systems differentiated overall by biochemical transformations, historically by biological processes, whose full description breaks up above all into species and their "differentially" individuated nitches and careers (*langues*) and ultimately into individual organisms with particular development and idiosyncracy.

In particular, a mammal, for example, has many innate tendencies to generalize environmental experience along various lines, particularly those aiding the mammal's survival. The chimpanzee "Washoe," for example, could be taught to recognize and correctly label quite new instances of cats, dogs, and birds (doubtless fruit kinds, too). And Washoe would have great trouble or find it impossible to generalize in other ways. But surely this must be true ("differentially") of mammals generally. So we might analogize these species-specific tendencies in generalization to the visual and language acquisition device (and other faculties) that we ascribe to humans. But of course members of mammal species are faced with varieties of habitats that will fill out in different ways this general and constraining program. (One might consider a cage habitat to represent some-

thing analogous to the habitat of "wild children," that is, children who pass through childhood without exposure to human language and socialization—certainly mammals brought up in cages find adjustment to more normal habitats nearly as impossible as have "wild children.")

Again, should one wish to cite an example with more social elements than those provided by a mammal family in which the immature species member is provided normal stimuli for full faculty development, one might consider the recent study of socialization, primarily status rankings, among macaques (Eaton, 1976). Macaque communities of several score members have peck rankings that are quite stable when once established through some initial confrontations as individuals mature and take a place in the order. One might consider that one has here a "differentiated" system of distinctions, an institution (*langue*) that exists apart from the actual physical characteristics of individuals and apart from their individual actions (*parole*) which may on occasion deviate from this system. One could even say that the "system" exists in the minds of the particular community of macaques. And this might seem to be a "differential" system that would rest on arbitrary social interactions rather than biologically programmed developments. But the case is thin if it is supposed to open some broad distinction in principle between biological and social science. The macaques, as a few other species of monkeys, are prone to develop such systems, and their survival is entangled with this proclivity. Further, the system of status distinctions has objective reality not only because human observers (or Siliconians) could come to describe it but in the sense that macaques are biologically programmed to socialize and mature into such a system of status niches. The differentiated tendency to aggressiveness and sense of personal status that each macaque comes to possess presumably must be represented at some level of brain biochemistry and so has as much physical reality in principle as simple strength, agility, or health, though of course it is not easily measured at present.

Second, even with respect to natural sciences such as physics and chemistry, the claim that natural sciences are exclusively concerned with "intrinsic properties of phenomena themselves,"

that for them "there is nothing corresponding to the distinction between *langue* and *parole*, there is no institution or system to be studied," is wholly dubious in that it is little more than a denial of realism about the theoretical–abstract, nonphenomenal, universal–entities and structures that seem to be the subject matter of physics and chemistry. We understand the scientific realist as one who tends to maintain that the unobserved entities and processes, abstract structures, laws, and natural kinds that scientific theories often seem to suggest are indeed real and not mere conveniences or contrivances that facilitate predictions about observables. The realist of the natural sciences champions the reality of unobservables such as electrons and protons, fields and forces, abstract structures, causes, and physical necessities, just as the realist in mathematics maintains that numbers and their properties exist apart from what we may know of them or as the realist in psychology maintains that there are minds and thoughts apart from observed human activity (similarly, I suggested that we take "human language is transformational-generative" and similar more particular generalizations about English to be statements about essential features of real things, human language and the English language, not mere convenient contrivances for expeditiously predicting specific pieces of human behavior). But, then, the scientific realist will of course distinguish and recognize various levels of abstraction in characterizing physical reality and thus will of course distinguish the accidental and more specific features of individuals (at various levels) from the systems and properties that these individuals realize.

Further, one might add that to insist that the natural sciences essentially study the "intrinsic properties of phenomena themselves" sounds like a pretwentieth if not prenineteenth-century view of natural science. It has certainly been fashionable for most of this Einsteinian century to stress that objects have properties such as color and even mass, velocity, and shape only in the context of a system of relationships which includes the observer. All one wants to insist upon is that the properties and systems that the linguist, the cognitive psychologist, or the universal structuralist social scientist wish to investigate are just as much a part of the fabric of reality as those that concern

the physical scientist or the biologist. Words, sentences, and languages are as real as any other things.

To sum up what seems most simply wrong with the position Culler puts forward, we can argue that it suggests that individual cultures section up and ascribe meanings to external reality in a wholly unique and arbitrary—Humpty-Dumpty—way: at one level an arbitrary set of phonemes (significant shapes, tastes, sounds, qualities, and so on), and at another a wholly arbitrary and local set of rules, meanings, concepts, and values. Rather, much of what we study in psychological and social science is more universal; and this more universal system underlies and makes possible a coherent characterization of local (and non-arbitrary) realizations of these universals on a group or individual level of description. It is revealing that the passage I quoted from Culler mentions natural and social science but leaves out biological and psychological science. As Levi-Strauss writes, "Structural thought now defends the cause of materialism. . . . Structuralism has only to be confronted with true manifestations of idealism and formalism for its own deterministic and realistic inspiration to become clearly manifest" (Levi-Strauss, 1969, p. 27; 1964, p. 35).

But the examples of visual and auditory perception, of facial recognition and linguistic faculties, are not the most contentious or difficult examples for universal structuralists. Why not ask whether we can hope to find, as Levi-Strauss suggests, universals in socialization, in eating and food preparation, in dress and deportment?

Though food and dress may seem rather unpromising subjects for the universal structuralist cognitive psychologist, they are universal and age-old concerns of humans, technologies as old as language itself; indeed, they are seemingly beneath study through their commonality, much as ordinary spoken language was until quite recently. Yet for all that, humans spend an enormous amount of time on such matters and often seem in possessing "taste" to have tacit knowledge of an extremely complicated sort. Levi-Strauss has remarked that food is to think with as much as to eat, with universalizing food metaphors reverberating through the whole of cultures and mythologies; and perhaps much the same is true of dress, which serves as

much to speak and cognize as to fend off rain or keep out cold.

I. Beeton, as one might expect of a nineteenth-century writer, finds cooking a theater of evolution and progress and a central work of civilization, though she also has a penchant for universalizing (Beeton, 1861).

> As in the fine arts, the progress of mankind from barbarism to civilization is marked by a gradual succession of triumphs over the rude materialities of nature, so in the art of cookery is the progress gradual from the earliest and simplest modes, to those of the most complicated and refined. Plain or rudely-carved stones, tumuli, or mounds of earth, are the monuments by which barbarous tribes denote the events of their history, to be succeeded, only in the long course of a series of ages, by beautifully-proportioned columns, gracefully-sculptured statues, triumphal arches, coins, medals, and the higher efforts of the pencil and the pen, as man advances by culture and observation to the perfection of his faculties. So it is with the art of cookery. Man, in his primitive state, lives upon roots and the fruits of the earth, until, by degrees, he is driven to seek for new means, by which his wants may be supplied and enlarged. He then becomes a hunter and a fisher. As his species increases, greater necessities come upon him, when he gradually abandons the roving life of the savage for the more stationary pursuits of the herdsman. These beget still more settled habits, when he begins the practice of agriculture, forms ideas of the rights of property, and has his own, both defined and secured. He sows and he reaps, pastures and breeds cattle, lives on the cultivated produce of his fields, and revels in the luxuries of the dairy; raises flocks for clothing, and assumes, to all intents and purposes, the habits of permanent life and the comfortable condition of a farmer. This is the fourth stage of social progress, up to which the useful or mechanical arts have been incidentally developing themselves, when trade and commerce begin. Accordingly, the art of cookery commences. Everything that is edible, and passes under the hands of the cook, is more or less changed, and assumes new forms. (p. 39)

And again,

> We have described the gradual progress of mankind in the art of cookery, the probability being, that the human race, for a long period, lived wholly on fruit. . . . It is natural that man should seek to feed on flesh; he has too small a stomach to be supported alone by fruit, which has not sufficient nournishment to renovate him (p. 257)

But this passage ends.

> Man's first weapons were the branches of trees, which were succeeded by bows and arrows, and it is worthy of remark, that these latter weapons have been found with the natives of all climates and latitudes. It is singular how this idea presented itself to individuals so differently placed.

Beeton, however, finally unites both the idea of progress and functionalism, and that of (species) universality in a remarkable passage:

> Man, it has been said, is a dining animal. Creatures of the inferior races eat and drink; man only dines. It has also been said that he is a cooking animal; but some races eat food without cooking it. A Croat captain said to M. Brillat Savarin, "When, in campaign, we feel hungry, we knock over the first animal we find, cut off a steak, powder it with salt, put it under the saddle, gallop over it for a half a mile, and then eat it." It is equally true that some races of men do not dine any more than the tiger or the vulture. It is not a *dinner* at which sits the aboriginal Australian, who gnaws his bone half bare and then flings it behind to his squaw. And the native of Terra-del-Fuego does not dine when he gets his morsel of red clay. Dining is the privilege of civilization. The rank which a people occupy in the grand scale may be measured by their way of taking their meals, as well as by their way of treating their women. The nation which knows how to dine has learnt the leading lesson of progress. It implies both the will and the skill to reduce to order, and surround with idealisms and graces, the more material conditions of human existence; and wherever that will and that skill exist, life cannot be wholly ignoble. (p. 905)

Though both agree in the importance it holds for understanding humanity, Beeton's interest respecting cooking in "the will and the skill to reduce to order, and surround with idealisms and graces" is practical and evolutionary (or culturely imperialist), while Levi-Strauss' is theoretical and committed to the belief that underlying properties of mind—Beeton's "idealisms and graces"—are universal, are "the same for ancient and modern, primitive and civilized" (Levi-Strauss, 1963, p. 20). Levi-Strauss begins his massive *Mythologiques* by writing "the aim of this

book is to show how empirical categories—such as the categories of the raw and the cooked, the fresh and the decayed, the moistened and the burned, etc., which can only be accurately defined by ethnographic observation and, in each instance, by adopting the standpoint of a particular culture—can nonetheless be used as conceptual tools with which to elaborate abstract ideas and combine them in the form of propositions" (1969, p. 1; 1964, p. 11). Cooking, whose conceptual reverberations or "idealisms and graces" are apparent in myths, is an essential route to mind:

> First of all, when considered from the formal point of view, myths which seem very different but all deal with the origin of man's mortality transmit the same message and can only be distinguished one from another by the code they use. Second, all the codes are similar in type; they use contrasts between tangible qualities, which are thus raised to the point of having a logical existence. Third, since man possesses five senses, there are five basic codes, which shows that all the empirical possibilities have been systematically explored and used. Fourth, one of the codes occupies a privileged position; this is the one connected with eating habits, the gustatory code, whose message is more often transmitted by the others than it is used to translate theirs, since it is through myths explaining the origin of fire, and thus of cooking, that we gain access to myths about man's loss of immortality. Among the Apinaye, for instance, the origin of mortality is only one episode of the myth relating to the origin of fire. We thus begin to understand the truly essential place occupied by cooking in native thought: not only does cooking mark the transition from nature to culture, but through it and by means of it, the human state can be defined with all its attributes, even those that, like mortality, might seem to be the most unquestionably natural. (Levi-Strauss, 1969, p. 164; 1964, p. 172)

As I have remarked, anything we would want to call a language, human or Siliconian, must be minimally logical and apt for communicating descriptions of the world. By the same token, the linguist is interested in the purely formal grammatical properties of language, those which reveal and follow from the peculiarities of the human mind. Similarly, Levi-Strauss is not interested in a practical or functionalist (or evolutionary) account of food gathering, preparation, or categorization. He is interested

in how humans think in or with food as revealed, for example, in the formal, mind-expressive aspects of myth—"myths signify the mind that evolves them by making use of the world of which it is itself a part: thus there is simultaneous production of myths themselves, by the mind that generates them and, by the myths, of an image of the world which is already inherent in the structure of mind" (Levi-Strauss, 1969, p. 341; 1964, p. 346).

Speaking of the calls uttered in South American Indian myth by rock and wood, Levi-Strauss writes, "They are operators, which makes it possible to convey the isomorphic character of all binary systems of contrasts connected with the senses and therefore to express a totality, a set of equivalences connecting life and death, vegetable foods and cannibalism, putrefaction and imputrescibility, softness and hardness, silence and noise" (Levi-Strauss, 1969, p. 153; 1964, p. 161). And the table he there provides gives graphic expression to these parallels:

code:	*auditory*	*gustatory*	*olfactory*	*tactile*
rock	loud call	cultivated plants	imputrescible	hard
hard wood		animal flesh		
rotten wood	faint call	human flesh	putrid	soft

What is one to make of this?

On the one hand, it is obvious that food preparation and the human sense of suitability for eating is extraordinarily complicated and as old and as basic as language, culture, or the peculiarities of human biology. And food metaphors and analogies reverberate prodigally in primitive myth and, for that matter, appear throughout literature with a profusion that rivals the sexual symbolism that has interested some psychologists. And it is obvious, *pace* Beeton, that humans have always surrounded cooking with profuse "graces and idealisms" quite apart from practical considerations as to the actual nourishment provided by various foods and the actual effect of various cooking

methods on the availability of this nourishment. So we have some warrant for speculating that "well-formed dishes," or suitably prepared suitable food, could be analogized to well-formed or grammatical sentences (words?, phonemes?). More expansively, a menu is like a grammar in that it specifies an ordered list of items with which to make an appropriate meal (the appetizers as articles, the fish course as nouns, the entrées as verbs, and desserts as adjectives, and the coffee as a period, and so on). Thus there is a syntax of dining (imagining the "well-formed" dishes as words or phonemes of this language of dining) and perhaps a semantics as well, since certain sequences of course items seem much the same while others are quite different, and since certain food selections "say" that one is a certain kind of person or in a certain position or mood. Clams casino, onion soup, baked potatoes and sour cream, and roast beef washed down with champagne conveys happiness and heartiness in a North American restaurant today much as would Beeton's nineteenth-century dinner of "soles á la Normandie, sweetbreads with sauce piquante, sirloin of beef, haunch of venison, fondue á la Brillat Savarin, and transparent jelly, inlaid with brandy cherries"—both would be inappropriate for a somber occasion or a cautious pose, quite apart from the actual biological appetite of the diner.

Further, it is suggestive that both primitive people and children appear to want to impose and preserve orders and categories in food quite apart from practical considerations. Mary Douglas, for example, is wholly convincing in her argument that the food prohibitions of Leviticus derive from a cognitive sense of "idealisms and graces": camel, pig, rock badger, and hare were supposed to violate the "normal" combination of cloven-hoof and cud-chewing; creatures that fly but have four legs are out; creatures of water that lack fins and scales are out; creatures that appear to use "hands" (not genuine forelegs) but walk on all fours are out—in general food should be orderly, properly categorized, separated, food "to think with" (Douglas, 1966). Thus it would seem with other systems of prohibitions. Indeed, the recent commitment to "natural" foods seems to derive from an abstract concern with order and separation, with idealisms and graces, as much as with any practical concern

with nutrition (many "health" foods are inferior or indistinguishable from their commercial forms in nutritional value). Similarly, children seem prone to separation and order in food as much as to familiarity and blandness; many children echo Wittgenstein's response, mentioned in N. Malcolm's *Memoir*, that anything was all right for breakfast so long as it was always the same. In *Uncle Wiggley* it is wholly natural that children should shun the scillary-scallery alligator who "likes soup cold and ice cream hot."

Similar points may be made about dress. Clothes have a syntax in that certain materials, textures, and colors are appropriate to specific body areas, quite apart from the practical consideration of the wear to which they are subject and the protection they are supposed to afford. And a person conveys a mode or pose through dress as much as through expression or manner. Despite Culler and Trubetzkoy this matter is not wholly local and arbitrary, both because one can understand how a culture teaches a special way of seeing clothes only through understanding how humans see and see clothes without such special instruction, and because aspects of our sense of clothes are universal (in what human culture does one cover more of the body with black clothing in order to suggest a happier and less formal mood and occasion?).

But there are problems in this investigation. Some stem from the lack of real study. Perhaps because of prejudice there simply is very little serious data on food and dress in a form apt to generalization and analysis. Other problems may derive from the subjects themselves.

The problems I would mention particularly are, first, that there is (in Levi-Strauss, for example) a lack of clarity about the levels of analysis; second, that there is a lack, whether remediable or not, of a large corpus of "well-formed dishes," or equivalents, from which to generalize; and, finally, the structures and units so far suggested are too finite and meager to allow the deep and testable mentalistic generalizations that linguistics or visual perception seem to afford us. These three problems are intertwined, since, for example, in linguistics it is the fact that native speakers agree on the well-formedness or grammaticality of a potentially infinitely large number of sen-

tences that allows the linguist to postulate, testably, that there are thus and so many levels of linguistic structure with units and rules for their generalization—and to ascribe a knowledge of these units and rules to the native speaker (and an acquisition capacity for this knowledge); for the native speaker can only know such a potentially number of structures through such an abstract, unconscious grasp of rules and abstract categories. That is, I am sure that all human cultures afford a notion of "well-formed dish" and of a "well-formed dish sequence" or complete meal, but I am not sure whether a "well-formed dish" is analogous to a phoneme, word, or sentence—not, of course, that I suppose that there is an exact analogy to linguistics, but that I am not sure what the relevant units and levels are. Are various taste parameters—salt, sour, sweet, and so on—like distinct features in phonology, a "complete unit of taste" being a combination of the presence and lack of various ones of these? (Odors will have to come in too. How?) Then a well-formed dish will be one or a combination of these that fit into a complete meal. But what of visual appearance and texture, or the actual materials and methods of preparation used? For surely, these determine how we understand a dish too. One is not sure how to individuate dishes, that is, how to distinguish the factors in their description, how to tell when one is meeting the same (kind of) dish or a variation of it.

But above all there is the apparant lack of a potentially infinite body of distinct, well-formed dishes or meals held in common by the dining community, as there is on the other hand among speakers of a human language agreement on a potentially infinite body of distinguishable sentences (as opposed to repetitions of individual sentences). Any competent speaker of English continually produces wholly new sentences (new structures rather than repetitions of old ones), confident that other speakers will recognize them as English. It is this fact that makes it necessary to suppose that speakers have a common and unconscious grasp of rules and abstract structures. If English consisted of a few thousand sentences we might suppose that speakers learned the sentences individually rather than learning rules and abstractions—or that speakers each had different rules or memory jogs, since a compact finite body of structures may

be generated by greatly varying sets of rules. But can we suppose that each dining culture shares a sense of a potentially infinite body of well-formed dishes or meals as opposed to mere repetitions? It is troublesome in this respect that Levi-Strauss deals with such a limited set of categories—raw, cooked, ashes, tobacco, honey, and so on—and nowhere suggests clearly what the requisite potentially infinite array might be.

As I have mentioned, Levi-Strauss analogizes his pursuit of cultural universals in an attempt to determine what pack a fortune-teller is using in telling a very large number of fortunes, given that the observer can only observe the person whose fortune is told and hear the fortune. Thus we might think of the myths as fortunes, the local natural circumstances as that whose fortune is told, and the cards themselves as mind, that is, as underlying human patterns of generalization. But while primitive peoples have languages which continually allow the common production and understanding of new sentences, they do not produce new "well-formed" myths with quite such prodigality. Levi-Strauss emphasizes the fact that the South American Indians he speaks of are happy to retell myths with minor creative variations; that is, they have a sense of what may be changed or played upon without malforming or changing the myth essentially. But it is not clear whether these are different tokens of one and the same structure—as people may say one and the same English sentence with variations in accent, pauses, pitch, and so on—or whether these are genuinely different types of a general sort of structure, types that must be generated separately and distinguishably by a grammar of myth. In general, the problem is that the Indians do not produce obviously new mythic structures daily, from time to time stumbling in creation, while other Indians are obviously and collectively cognizant that a malformed or ungrammatical myth has been uttered (that is, *not* a bad reproduction of an old myth but a new myth which, as opposed to other new myths, violates the tacit, underlying rules of myth making shared by the tribal community, just as an ungrammatical sentence would violate their shared linguistic sense). Again, the myth investigator, unlike the language investigator, is apparently not in a position to produce new myths to which natives will easily and quickly react with uniform

judgments of mal- or well-formedness; and accordingly the myth investigator may not gradually test out various hypotheses as to the rules needed to generate such a potentially infinite body of "well-formed" myths.

In the four volumes of *Mythologiques* Levi-Strauss investigates some several hundred myths that are found through tribes stretching over much of the American continent, with no more than a score belonging to any individual tribal group or myth community. It is hard not to think that this set of samples cannot be enough. Since Levi-Strauss seems more than conscious of the technical demands of his undertaking (Levi-Strauss, 1955) we may certainly call his work suggestive. But the problem of the general lack of formalization in *Mythologiques* does seem extremely serious. In his classic, *The Elementary Structures of Kinship* (1949), Levi-Strauss works with the more well-defined notion of well- or mal-formed marriage and extracts from varying kinships systems something like a universal sense of what constitutes a distinctive feature of a relation of kinship and of what can be a possible rule of kinship, thus understanding each kinship system that has occurred as a selection from a highly constrained set of "humanly possible" or "humanly learnable" kinship systems (as opposed to vast numbers of impossible and arbitrary kinship systems). Indeed, Levi-Strauss adds to one chapter of *The Elementary Structures of Kinship* an appendix by the mathematician André Weil giving a complex algebraic analysis of the Australian Murngin marriage laws.

It is a measure of the obscurity, whether removable or not, of these matters that one has no idea of what sort of mathematics, what sort of formalization, might be relevant to the generation of "well-formed dishes," "well-formed dresses," or "well-formed myths." In the case of language, we have the familiar apparatus of recursive function theory: we know the solution lies somewhere between the power of unrestricted transformations and context-sensitive phrase structure rules, and we know how to write grammars. In the case of visual perception we have the general mathematics of topology with which to express the difference between a human grasp of a scene, the human tendency to generalize certain patterns and ignore others, and so on, as against a camera's neutrality. But I, at least, have

no idea of where one goes with food, dress, and myth. Still, considering the centrality of these in our common existence I find it impossible not to think that something of great depth and importance will be found in these areas, and something extraordinarily intriguing as well, something of Beeton's "graces and idealisms" with which "life cannot be wholly ignoble."

CHAPTER 5

Universal Structuralism and the Waning of the Game Metaphor

WRITERS, occupations, interest groups, cultures, indeed, whole eras, have characteristic metaphors. Though such characteristic metaphors serve such groups in self-understanding, or at least self-satisfaction, these metaphors at the same time reveal much about the basic presumptions and fears of such groups. Thomas Hobbes, for example, was echoing his approval of monarchy and the spirit of his age when he compared a state to a Leviathan, a gigantic biological organism within which some would have the natural function of command while others as naturally would serve as muscles or messengers—that the people and the provinces should obey the sovereign would be as natural and as healthy as that one's leg muscles should move when one is of a mind to walk. When John Locke replaced this model by analogizing the state to a contractual and voidable agreement among equal and self-sufficient individuals for the more regular administration of justice, he was echoing the rising commercial, capitalist, and antifeudal interests of his age and social class. I would say that the commanding metaphor of our age is the game. To say that something is like a game or is a game is everywhere regarded as a crucial route to understanding one or another aspect of some segment of our existence and activity.

What is less remarked is that this metaphor, as past characteristic metaphors, serves to rationalize and reinforce various interests and prejudices: equally, the various uses of the game metaphor reveal the characteristic intellectual and ethical attitudes of this century. In particular, I think that the game metaphor reveals a general skeptical and decadent attitude that is specifically realized in relativistic structuralism and elsewhere

in our cultural milieu. With the specific difficulties that have called explicit relativistic structuralism in question, we also find the waning of the game metaphor.

What I want to do in this concluding chapter is to trace some of the ramifications and spiritual underpinnings of the game metaphor—its multifaceted career through our century. This will allow me once more to review the conflict between relativistic and universal structuralism. It will also allow me to say something—I hope not so much as to vex the reader—about the temper of our time. What I do hope to show is that there is a connection between such far-ranging phenomena as Von Neumann and Morgenstern's "theory of games," a mathematical theory of strategy with applications to the "games" of marketing, collective bargaining, war, and other conflict situations; psychological theories such as Eric Berne's, which unmask human interactions as *Games People Play*; philosophers' attempts to understand logic, mathematics, and language (if not ethics and social life) as the playing of various games; and so on. What so often happens is that the use of the game metaphor, the claim that *this is like a game*, is supposed to aid understanding, is supposed to remove false hopes, superstitions, naiveté, and sentimental prejudice. What I want to suggest is that the very use of the metaphor, the insistence that it brings understanding, can help our understanding of the attitudes, assumptions, and aims of those who use the metaphor.

In *N-Person Game Theory*, Anatol Rapoport, for example, writes:

> The origins of game theory stem from concerns related to rational decisions in situations involving conflicts of interest. The term game theory itself derives from the analysis of so-called *games of strategy* such as chess, bridge, etc. Serious research in this area was doubtlessly stimulated by a need to bring to bear the power of rigorous analysis on problems faced by persons in the culturally dominant roles of "decision makers." That connections between games of strategy and strategic conflict already exist in the minds of men of affairs appears in the metaphors linking the languages of business, international relations, and war. . . . In short, the game metaphor (business is a game, life is a game, politics is a game) is already firmly established among people whose careers depend on the choice

of right decisions and among those who have an appreciation of this process. (p. 45)

Parenthetically, the use of "game" to mean one's occupation, profession, or job is of twentieth-century origin. The *Oxford English Dictionary*, among others, does not give such a use prior to recent decades. Indeed, according to this dictionary, the notion of "playing the game" as equivalent to "abiding by the basic ethical commitments of one's community" first appeared in English in 1889. In short, while Rapoport may be right in thinking that the metaphor has been "firmly established" among those "persons in the culturally dominant roles of 'decision makers'" even prior to Von Neumann's original work, the metaphor has become commonplace only in this century. In short, the Victorians thought that "life is earnest, life is real"; they thought that war and business were at best crusades for progress, welfare, and enlightenment, or, at worst, reversions to savagery and immorality—not the cool and morally neutral, rule-bound conflict between those who "play the game," who accept without question *and without responsibility* the arbitrary and conventional rules of their culture or occupation.

What, then, is implied by saying that something—"business," "life," "politics," war, ethics, or whatever—is a game? What attitude are we being invited to take up by the metaphor? What is it about actual games such as chess or bridge that the use of the metaphor invites us to read into activities that are not, literally, games?

There are six related characteristics of games that seem important to many uses of the game metaphor, that is, six characteristics of games which those who use the game metaphor want us to see in phenomena that are not, literally, games—characteristics that we are supposed to be blind to unless the metaphor shakes us out of our ordinary and troubling way of seeing things. Through the metaphor we are to learn that "the riddle does not exist." Through the metaphor we are to "shake off the picture that holds us captive" and end our "bewitchment by language," by those features of our thinking and speaking that mask gamelike characteristics of our activities. In part these six characteristics are just those that the relativistic structuralist

draws to our attention in the relativistic structuralist's analysis of the phenomena of the human sciences. Here I will list and review these characteristics. I want to show that there is a substantial continuity among superficially unrelated uses of the game metaphor.

(1) *Games, in particular the rules that constitute them, are arbitrary, artificial, and local.* By the same token games and their rules are not universal or "natural," not part of the fabric of reality studied by the "natural sciences." Ludwig Wittgenstein, for example, was at one time worried as to why the "truths" of pure logic and mathematics are true (and consistent, and so on). Particularly in the 1920s, he came to feel that his worries arose from a false picture of things. He came to say that logical and mathematical "truths" are a matter of the conventions we adopt, that there are indefinitely many "games" of logic and mathematics that we can play. He supposed that there could be no question as to whether any mathematical system (or game) is true or even inconsistent in and of itself: these questions could only be asked in the context of another system or game, with the answer depending on what game one decided to play (*Philosophical Remarks*, 1974, appendix 2). More generally, many philosophers and psychologists have been inclined to think that many philosophical or psychological "questions" are bogus and misleading. These questions (like questions about mathematics and logic) may appear to be factual questions like those of the natural sciences, but instead they are a product of confusion and misanalogy—in effect, one is questioning the rules or conventions of a game (a calculus, a language) as if these rules could be true or false and as if they were something other than the rules of a game. Many have shared Wittgenstein's notion that asking about the nature of numbers, concepts, theoretical entities, or the meanings of words—asking as to what is possible or necessary—is like asking about the nature of a piece such as the queen in chess (I shall return to this comparison which I first introduced on page 30).

(2) *Games, in particular the rules that constitute them, are taught to those who play them.* Game rules are accessible to the consciousness of those who play, and we would not say that a person was playing the game or following its rules unless

the teaching of the rules and the (potential) consciousness of them had a role in that person's actions. This point, which may be thought to follow from (1), metaphorically legislates an empiricist theory of knowledge. If, for example, mathematics, language, or politics are games, that is, are arbitrary, conventional, and artificial, then they must be taught to anyone who knows or plays them. What has been taught is accessible to the consciousness of the individual who has learned, and *to explain how the rule*, the piece of knowledge of mathematics, language, or politics, *is taught is to explain in what the rule or knowledge consists.* Hence, and here is the critical bite, what is not taught explicitly, what is not accessible to consciousness for explicit consultation, is not known, is not part of the game of mathematics, language, or politics. An extreme example would be Wittgenstein's claim that "there are no *hidden* contradictions in mathematics" (Wittgenstein, 1974, appendix 2). A commonplace example would be the claim of many philosophers and a few linguists that something can only be a rule or feature of a human language as it is known by a particular speaker if it was explicitly learned by the individual and is accessible to that individual's consciousness. Such adherents of the game metaphor are inclined to hold that the very idea of humans having innate knowledge of the universal features of human language is senseless, since what is innate cannot be taught and what is universal cannot belong to a game (to the subject matter of a human science). Indeed, the game metaphor suggests that the idea of unconscious or untaught knowledge is wholly senseless.

Existentialism as a stylish philosophical movement echoed this view in insisting that the essence of human nature was to have no nature. Anything relevant to humans as humans, as political and ethical beings, as the subject matter of the human sciences, would be learned, chosen, and accessible to consciousness, local to a culture or an individual life. But much more simply, there is the view of behaviorists like Skinner, relativist structuralists, and many other psychological scientists that psychology and the human sciences generally are wholly and solely concerned with what is local and what is learned. What is neither learned nor local, what is not accessible to consciousness and wholly derived from conscious experience, simply does not

belong to the human existence that is the subject matter of psychology and the human sciences. (Of course, one cannot resist adding that one of the most striking features of ["the game of"] real life as opposed to literal games is that one neither chooses to enter real life or leave it, and that in real life one is continually affected by realities that are not announced in rule books, that one frequently discovers hidden features, if not "contradictions," of this existence.)

(3) *Rules (and the games that they constitute) are not true or false, natural or unnatural, moral or immoral.* Wittgenstein relieved his puzzles about the status of mathematical and logical "truths" or "proofs" by regarding them as games. Somewhat similarly, some radical empiricists who have worried about the status of scientific "laws" or probability statements have wanted to avoid realism by claiming that such assertions are not true or false but are rather rules of good strategy or good betting. Further, some have wanted to say that it is senseless and misleading to ask whether certain social "rules" or customs are natural or unnatural, moral or immoral, true or false. Such "rules" constitute "the game" of a particular culture or society. One can no more meaningfully debate whether a particular rule is moral or immoral, true or false, than one can meaningfully debate whether the rule of chess that indicates that the king may move one square in any direction is moral or immoral, true or false. Of course, one can ask whether or not some "constitutive" rule *is* a rule of a particular society, just as one can ask whether the rule I have given for the movement of the king *is* a rule of chess. But, so the metaphor is intended to suggest, *there is no further question to be asked.*

(4) The meaning, particularly the "evaluative" meaning, of "moves" in a game *are all internal* to the game. Since the rules that constitute the game are arbitrary and local conventions, it follows that disputes about the significance of various actions ("moves") are only resolvable by consulting such conventions—appeals to "brute natural facts" that transcend the game, such as human suffering or the material interests of those who formulate or support "the rules" are ruled out. The thesis that the significance and evaluative meaning of the "moves" are all internal to the conventions of the game equally may be put by

saying that the same arbitrary conventions that constitute the game at the same time constitute the vocabulary for describing, understanding, or evaluating the game. The rules of the game wholly close the question as to what is meant by plays, by allowable or fair, by winning or losing, and by shrewd play. (It is, in effect, a cool technical problem to determine what is good strategy once the rules have been laid down, what is an allowable move, and what constitutes winning.)

"Ordinary language" or "speech act" philosophers of recent decades have gone far in understanding all human action, particularly speech action or the "performative" aspect of language, as belonging to various human games whose rules for play are *at the same time* linguistic conventions through which we understand what the plays mean. Consequently, the writings of philosophers of speech acts often suggest that to have learned to speak a human language is at the same time to have learned and accepted a mass of conventions that specify what one has done, what obligations and responsibilities one has undertaken, in activities as diverse as betting, promising, ordering, contracting, questioning, requesting, exorcising, umpiring, judging, sentencing, appointing, and so on. To speak the language and to put oneself and others under the rule of countless social "games" are one and the same.

Though this belongs as much to the fifth aspect of the game metaphor, I might here add that John Searle, for example, has argued that *as a matter of the "rules" of the English language* to say "I promise to pay you five dollars"—given circumstances specified by the "rules" of English—is to promise to pay you five dollars; and that this means, again by the "rules" of English, that I ought, that I have moral obligations, to pay you five dollars. Similarly, one imagines that Searle ought to hold that if the year is 1800 and I say "I sell you this slave Charlie for five dollars" and you pay me five dollars, it follows by the rules of English that you own Charlie and that you and Charlie ought, or have the moral obligation, to conduct yourselves in accord with the master-slave game. The notion that the "rules" of various activities such as ordering, promising, betting, arguing, postulating, baptizing, and so on, are all "rules of the English language" is another version of the notion that all of culture

is one language, that all conceptual, theoretical, and moral truths are constituted in the fabric of the "prison" of one's native language. It is helpful to remind oneself that it is quite alien to the prudent linguist's notion of linguistic competence as to what is *common* to the speakers of a particular human language. Obviously, if one wants to know about betting, ordering, exorcising, or sentencing, one should consult a bettor, officer, priest, or judge, respectively, whatever the native language of these individuals with special, nonlinguistic competencies. While promising, requesting, predicting, and so on, are done by all who speak, they raise moral, social, and cognitive problems that have little to do with the particular competencies of a speaker of English. One can know as much as there is to be known about promising, requesting, and predicting without speaking a word of English, just as one can know all about lions, numbers, or atoms without knowing the English (or Turkish) words for these things.

(5) There is little or no place for the ordinary or traditional notion of moral and immoral in literal games. There is a place for shrewdness and skill in the sorts of games (chess, bridge, poker, and so on) that those who use the game analogy have in mind. But, as in (4), the notions of winning and losing, of "good"—that is, winning—play are all defined within the rules of the game. The shrewdness and skill, then, are in effect without the responsibility often felt respecting such qualities in real life. "It is only a game," we say to the loser who is so unruly as to let emotion show. "I totally destroyed Jones" is natural to the lips of the winner at chess, and such a remark is hardly the offense to conscience that it would be were the circumstance a tenure decision that came to mean the end of Jones' career.

In everyday life moral questions come up when one stands a chance to gain, at least materially, at some cost to the interests and needs of others. What we or traditional moralists regard as the proper attitude is something like one of the following: act in a principled and fair fashion so as not to regard your own interests and needs as having a more important status than those of others; act to maximize the happiness of those concerned (without, that is, giving your own happiness special status), or,

simply, love others as yourself. By saying "It's only a game," we mean to call attention to two features in which literal games (mostly) are not like real life. (*A*) There is supposed to be little (or no) "moral" dimension of assessment in the sense I have sketched. There are to be winners and losers and the winners are not supposed to grieve—a game with welfare benefits or charity (perhaps for those not in "the culturally dominant roles of 'decision makers' "?) to prevent potential losers from really losing would not be a game. (*B*) Notions such as "interests and needs," "happiness," "love," that belong to moral assessment are not supposed to be arbitrary, local, or conventional, nor necessarily clearly understood by everyone: they are universal and natural. One *can* always say "By the conventions of the game *Careers* (or whatever), Joe is 'happy' but in fact he is not." One cannot make sense in saying "By the rules of chess Joe has by his move checkmated his opponent but in fact he has not checkmated his opponents."

As a child I once made the mistake of ignoring feature (*A*). I "forgot" that I was playing a game. My father and I were playing *Monopoly.* After some time I had "bought" and "improved with hotels" most of the "property" on the board. When my father's token finally landed on the property that would result in a ruinous, game-ending "rent," I tried to give him "money" and broke down into tears when he refused it. Hardly the proper attitude for a game player—or for those "in the culturally dominant roles of 'decision makers.' " Benjamin Franklin (as one infatuated with the game analogy) might be said to have made the reverse mistake in his *Autobiography.* There he speaks of maintaining his press' reputation for economy by pushing a cart through Philadelphia every month (though he had had enough success by that time that he did no other hard physical labor). After recounting this "playful" ruse, he notes with evident satisfaction and not the slightest sign of compassion that his competitor was "sold into debtor's slavery in the Barbadoes." I am inclined to feel happier with someone who makes the mistake in the direction I took.

(6) Games are not serious, not fatal; a cool, calculating, detached attitude is appropriate in that "It's only a game." Of course, as I have already suggested, this belongs more to a

certain idealization of the notion of games. It explains something about what those who use the metaphor are after, not about actual games. Indeed, in this age of the game metaphor it would appear that literal games often capture our imagination more than "real life" itself. Successful players are the natural aristocrats of our age. Martin Shubik remarks of those who played a game created to exemplify situations to which the mathematical theory of games might most clearly apply, "The four inventors of the game still occasionally talk to each other" (Rapoport, p. 283). Emanuel Lasker, the world chess champion for the first two decades of this century and a professor of philosophy, found in the literal game to which he devoted much of his life an exemplification of the Darwinian struggle which characterized human existence in general. Once games lose their characteristic status as momentary respites from real life, they seem to shed the features I have listed.

In short, the game metaphor calls our attention to aspects of real life that are like games, since games, and the rules that constitute them, are (1) arbitrary, artificial, and local and (2) taught to those who play them and hence accessible to consciousness; and (3) the rules of games are not true or false, natural or unnatural, moral or immoral. In particular, (4) the meaning of "moves" in games normally are internal to the arbitrary game conventions; (5) even within such games there is no place for a dimension analogous to ordinary moral assessment; and (6) the appropriate emotional attitude for players is coolness. (Another way to put [4] is to say that the rules are understood to provide the essential language, the semantics, for describing what goes on in the game, for the language and the game are one.)

In using the game metaphor one is suggesting that one, many, or all of these features are present in what is literally not a game. If anything is central to the unease of one who seeks relief in the game metaphor it is that something crucial—human existence, mathematics, language itself, social life, morality, aesthetics, political and economic life, and so on—has no universality, has no real, substantial mooring in the nature of reality or in human nature. The metaphor says: your unease is pointless, for what worries you has no such mooring, nor needs

it—there is nothing more than game conventions which are local to those who play this particular game or use its language, and which neither needs, nor affords, a larger mode of assessment. Certainly what I have called relativistic structuralism finds the game metaphor apt in this sort of way.

There are all too many historical reasons why people have felt the unease to which the metaphor ministers. Materially, there is the loss of confidence in European civilization, in progress, in the world role of white, Christian Europe. World War I, the Great Depression, the decline and unmasking of colonial empires, Soviet Russia, whose development came to demoralize the left to the degree that it horrified the right—all these came to shake the confidence that had been the product of a hundred years of European peace and success. Intellectually, the revolution in modern physics seemed to suggest that the universe was not a Newtonian one, governed by a few inexorable laws that were agreeable to human reason; rather, random movement appeared at the base of a structure that seemed quite alien, even inconceivable, to human reason. Darwinian biology insisted that the human species was one among the other animal kinds thrown up by natural selection, an uninspired offshoot of the anthropoid apes that had existed only for a tiny portion of the earth's biological history. Modern psychology, following Freud, suggested that human behavior and thought—indeed, morality, conscience, guilt—were by-products of irrational, savage, and instinctual processes, inacessible and frightening to the conscious mind, which itself came to seem more the rationalizer and gullible dissembler for unconscious drives than the master of its fate. Sociology and anthropology suggested that human communities had quite various conceptions of morality and rationality, just as the study of languages suggested that societies might not simply act differently but might also think and understand the world each in its own conceptual prison. All the human sciences contrived to suggest that Christianity was but one of a vast and mutually incompatible collection of religious systems, each obviously arising from the peculiar needs and local situation of various cultures. Finally, economics and history seemed to suggest the fragility, transience, or duplicity of the

general sort of politico-economic system that had been thrown up in the course of European history.

In philosophy as an academic and intellectual discipline one finds reflections of all these changes. Traditionally, philosophy had sought to understand the most general truths about nature and our place in it. Such philosophy had asked what general sorts of things there were in the universe, in what we know in general about these things, and in what we should in general do about them. Such philosophy had seemed to rest in the main on the most general truths of science. But in this century many philosophers came to feel that traditional philosophy had consisted, on the one hand, of actual scientific questions which could be left to actual scientific research, since they only *seemed* to have philosophic significance. On the other hand, such philosophers thought that the rest of traditional philosophy consisted of questions which seemed to be about the "deeper" features of reality but were mere confusions that could be removed by careful attention to *either* the conventions (the games) that were only the logical skeleton for stating real scientific truths *or* the "linguistic" conventions that were only the local and arbitrary cultural scaffolding for carrying on the countless games of social existence (Ludwig Wittgenstein brought the game metaphor to bear as a major figure in both of these variations in "linguistic" philosophy). Briefly, philosophy could not seek a mooring in the "deeper features of reality," for there were no such features. The illusion that there were such features could be removed by careful attention to the role of logico-linguistic conventions—could be removed by again and again bringing those bemused by philosophical questions to see the gamelike aspects of our existence.

But as time went on further research—less playful science—showed in case after case that what one had wanted to understand as a game, as a set of local and consciously accessible conventions without a substantial and universal dimension of assessment as true or false, moral or immoral, turned out to have such dimensions. It became impossible to maintain the neo-Burkean notion of natureless humans, constituted by indoctrination within countless local and arbitrary, equally valid, games. Neither logic and mathematics, nor natural language or

human thought, could be understood as mere games. The whole picture suggested by the game metaphor has been gradually turned inside out. Human beings are understood again to share a substantial common nature, but this nature is significantly mental and abstract—humans think the same as much as they have a common gross physical nature. (My invented title—"universal structuralism"—emphasizes that recent thinking in the psychological sciences is a pursuit of what is common to humans and after what is mental.)

I will sketch the reversals that have led to the waning of the game metaphor, moving from the more impersonal subjects such as mathematics and logic to subjects such as ethics and religion—and finally the moral.

Recall that Wittgenstein, together with many other mathematical logicians, was worried about the basis for mathematics, about its consistency and truth, and had wanted to say that there were no hidden contradictions in mathematics, that there was no such thing as absolute inconsistency or falsity in a mathematical calculus. A calculus—and here the game metaphor is introduced—may only be seen to be "inconsistent" *within* another calculus (or consistent within yet another). In general, Wittgenstein thought that logical and mathematical truths were true by convention, the upshot of the adoption of a calculus. Thus to lay down a calculus, a mathematical system, is like inventing a game. Asking what the number three is is like asking what the queen is in chess. A proof in a mathematical system is like a sequence of moves that the rules of the game allow.

Now it is true that the queen in chess can be regarded as an abstract object, one defined through the rules of the game. But the comparison breaks down. It breaks down—it was seen to break down in the first three decades of this century—in two related ways.

In order to fill out the comparison a bit, suppose we say that the rules of chess specify the very large number of possible sequences of moves (particular games), starting from the opening position and ending in checkmate (a win for white or black) or stalemate (a tie in which either one side has no legal moves or there has been a repetition of the same position three times). Now we can take the white queen and the other pieces to be

the abstract objects whose nature is wholly specified in indicating how they fit into these sequences. (Note that the reason I call them abstract objects is that a particular sequence—for example Andersson's famous "Evergreen" game of 1852—might be represented by pieces of different patterns, shapes, colors, sizes, or by various notations, diagrams, and so on. Note also that, given the rules and particularly the provision for stalemate by repetition of position, all chess games have to be of finite length and surveyable number of games. Note, finally, that I am ignoring the fact that many chess players stop playing before they have finished a game either because there is no more time or because the eventual outcome is reasonably clear.)

Correspondingly, we can imagine that mathematical objects and operations are specified in saying that we take the axioms, definitions, and proof procedures to be rules that specify possible proofs ("games"), and we take whatever we take mathematics to be true of, or represented by, to correspond to all the ways of representing particular games. If what we think represents our "game-mathematics"—for example, that actual space is a representation of Euclidean geometry—turns out not to do so, then we choose not to say that our "game-mathematics" is false but that our representation assignment was inappropriate. Perhaps we might imagine Wittgenstein's late 1920s notion of inconsistency to be realized if one supposed that there was a position respecting which the rules would suggest both that the game had ended and that it had not, or that the position was both a win for black and for white.

The now familiar first problem with the game metaphor is that it has been established that the "rules" (axioms and so on of basic mathematical logic) cannot prove all of the truths that we know must be true of what mathematical logic and arithmetic are about. There are logical formulas (or equivalent arithmetical equations) that we know are true in any standard model, any representation, of mathematical logic that cannot be provided on pain of inconsistency. Thus what basic mathematics and logic are about must be real, must be independent of formal or conventional attempts to specify its nature by fiat.

If logic and mathematics were a game, we might then decide to change the rules (indeed, fragments of basic mathematical

logic are complete and some are even surveyable in the way that chess is). Thus in chess the rule that calls a game a tie or stalemate undoubtedly arose because a chess position came up in which one rule said that one side had to move, it being that side's turn, while another rule said that that side's only possible moves were not allowable because they would move that side's king into check. Similarly, the draw by repetition of position rule arose because it was noticed that otherwise a game could go on forever. If the rules of chess produce a "contradictory" result that we do not like, we change them; if the rules do not terminate all games in a finite number of moves, we arbitrarily decide on three (not four, five, and so on) as the number that terminates the game by repetition of position. Thus someone who really believed mathematical logic to be a game might suggest we should confine it to a complete, finitely decidable format. But—and this is the second defect in the game metaphor—we have an independent sense of what we want to be true in mathematical logic (truths which are everywhere in the sciences and more central than any others). It is as if all the possible games of chess existed in independence and priority to the invention and compilation of the rules, which then would be mere descriptions, true or false, of the logically prior games. But—particularly since the so-called "game rules" of mathematics and logic would describe not merely chess pieces but all the contents of the universe and perhaps all possible universes as well—in that case all of the gamelike characteristics drop out of the picture. What we have is *not* (1), local, arbitrary, or conventional; *not* (2), wholly learned in the sense of requiring explicit training as something that is not universal to normal human mental development; and, respecting the "rules" that comprise mathematical logic, *not* (3), something that has no (semantic) dimension of truth or falsity or (4), that can make "true," "consistent," and "complete" mean whatever is stipulated.

In Chapter 3 I showed that essentially the same situation obtains in linguistics and in significant parts of cognitive psychology. A natural language cannot be gamelike, since (1) it has many universal phonological, syntactic, and semantic features and presupposes common infinitistic tendencies in generalizing; (2) the part of it which is learned cannot be learned without

sizable innate linguistic knowledge (nor is much of our deeper linguistic knowledge transparent to consciousness); (3) there are severe limitations on what can be a genuine rule of grammar even among those compatible with the linguist's data; and (4) terms like "phoneme," "word," "noun," "sentence," "rule of grammar," and so on do not mean whatever we arbitrarily stipulate (that is, linguists can, indeed have, discovered that the phenomena designated by these terms are not what previous linguists, or language-users, thought they meant). Similarly, while particular cultures may crudely block or add a certain veneer to cognitive activities such as visual perception, facial recognition, even perhaps understanding of food, dress, and sexuality, we cannot genuinely understand these cultural interventions except within the context of a rich, universal, largely unconscious and untaught natural human endowment. The human being is not a blank tablet on which some local culture, language, or set of games etches its peculiar system or conceptual prison. The human being is a collection of substantially innate competencies, fleshed out with local influences, particular experiences, and so on.

Within philosophy itself there has been an outward turning and a renewal of ties with empirical science. Philosophers who used the game metaphor inherited the tradition of methodological skepticism and the search for necessary, a priori or certain truths. As I mentioned in Chapter 2, Wittgenstein marshalled an argument against any private, phenomenal language and insisted that our common ability to speak with each other, to know how to go on with the fragments of language or other experiences of our cognitive development, must rest on regularities in human psychology, in the world, in social situations. But he had no real interest as a philosopher in what these regularities were in particular, nor as to which were social, which natural, which essential, which statistical.

However, there is no reason not to return to the older philosophical tradition that had such interests—interests in questions about the particular character of the basic propositions of the sciences and in questions about the general character of the reality that these sciences uncover. As I have suggested, the universe of particular, contingent facts, expressed within local conventions, cannot be our universe, nor can it serve as a basis

for a cognitive psychology of competence which will be moored in necessary features of the world to which our minds have essential access. We have come to understand both of the world and of the mind that our vocabulary is referential, is essentially not stipulative but responsive to discovery and theory. But if the human mind has a common, deep, and discoverable set of faculties, not accessible, with privilege, to ordinary individual consciousness if accessible at all to consciousness—if the mind is naturalized—then it is at least possible that the moral and political perceptions of individual human communities may themselves be just peculiar fleshings out of an underlying human faculty for moral and political understanding.

A Wittgensteinian philosopher might respond by saying, "Perhaps all humans happen to think this way, or that way; perhaps their happening to think this or that way may be a psychological or even biological necessity of normal human development; but what is this to me as a philosopher? This will in no way tell me how any thinking being must think, nor how the world must be for any thinking being (or any being that possesses a language adequate to the description of the universe)—nor will it minister to the problems raised by the Cartesian tradition of methodological doubt, for the necessities do not belong, nor can be seen as necessary, to the ordinary conscious mind."

I mentioned in the preface that I might have used the label "empiricism" for "relativistic structuralism" and "rationalism" for "universal structuralism" if I had wanted to emphasize the strands of continuity between some of this century's conflicts in the psychological sciences and those of the seventeenth and eighteenth centuries. One reason I did not wish to emphasize that continuity is that two features have dropped out that were central to the older debate. First, it is now wholly implausible to think that mind (or cognitive psychology) is transparently accessible, or in the main accessible at all, to individual human consciousness. Second, it is now implausible to suppose that any (finite) thinking being thinks as humans do (even if there are not any Siliconians there certainly might be such). Perhaps what has made this change seem plausible is that computation and computer theory have begun to make it clear that there are various kinds of thinking, that is, various kinds of software,

each of which may have realization in quite varied hardware, and has also made it clear that one can talk coherently about the software of a thinking device without supposing that the software is introspectively available. In any case, one reason I kept the term "structuralism" was to emphasize the self-reflectiveness or sophistication of recent psychology—that is, that the *species* of thinker, the human mind, has moved to center stage, distinguished from the thinker as any rational being or from the thinker as the conscious mind of the philosopher-psychologist. As Wittgenstein himself came to fully realize, the central Cartesian problem of the seventeenth and eighteenth centuries could not, cannot, be answered on its own terms. The human mind is in the world.

Selected Bibliography

AUSTIN, J. L. *Philosophical Papers*. Oxford: Oxford University Press, 1962.

BACH, EMMON. *Syntactic Theory*. New York: Holt, Rinehart, and Winston, 1974.

BARTHES, ROLAND. "Science versus Literature." *Times Literary Supplement*, September 28, 1967.

BEETON, I. *The Book of Household Management*. London: S. O. Beeton, 1861.

BLOOMFIELD, L. *Language*. New York: Holt, Rinehart, and Winston, 1933.

BOWER, T. "The Object in the World of the Infant." *Scientific American*, October, 1971.

BRESNAN, J. "Sentence Stress and Syntactic Transformations." In *Approaches to Natural Language*, edited by Hintikka. Dordrecht: D. Reidel, 1973.

CHOMSKY, N. *Syntactic Structures*. The Hague: Mouton, 1957.

———. *Aspects of the Theory of Syntax*. Cambridge, Mass.: MIT Press, 1965.

———. *Reflections on Language*. New York: Pantheon Books, 1975.

———. *Studies on Semantics in Generative Grammar*. The Hague: Mouton, 1972.

———, and HALLE, M. *The Sound Pattern of English*. New York: Harper & Row, 1968.

DE GEORGE, R. T., and DE GEORGE, F. M., eds. *The Structuralists*. New York: Doubleday, 1972.

DOUGLAS, MARY. *Purity and Danger*. London: Routledge & Kegan Paul, 1966.

EATON, G. "The Social Order of Japanese Macaques." *Scientific American*, October, 1976.

HARRIS, Z. *Methods in Structural Linguistics*. Chicago: University of Chicago Press, 1951.

ISAAC, G. "Stages of Cultural Elaboration in the Pleistocene: Possible Archaeological Indicators of the Development of Language Capabilities." New York Academy of Sciences Conference on Origins and Evolution of Language and Speech, September 23, 1975.

Katz, J. J. *Semantic Theory.* New York: Harper & Row, 1972.

Kiparsky, P. "Linguistic Universals and Language Change." In *Universals in Linguistic Theory,* edited by E. Bach and R. Harms. New York: Holt, Rinehart, and Winston, 1972.

Kripke, S. "Naming and Necessity." In *Semantics of Natural Language,* edited by D. Davidson and G. Harman. Dordrecht: D. Reidel, 1972.

Lakoff, George. "Linguistics and Natural Logic." In *Semantics of Natural Language,* edited by D. Davidson and G. Harman. Dordrecht: D. Reidel, 1972.

Lenneberg, E. *Biological Foundations of Language.* New York: John Wiley & Sons, 1967.

Levi-Strauss, C. *The Elementary Structures of Kinship.* Boston: Beacon Press, 1969. The original first edition was published in 1949.

———. *Structural Anthropology.* New York: Basic Books, 1963. Translation of the 1958 publication.

———. *The Raw and the Cooked.* New York: Harper & Row, 1969. Translation of *Le Cru et le Cuit* (1964). This and the subsequent three volumes of *Mythologiques* have been published by Librairie Plon, Paris.

Peters, S., and Ritchie, R. W. "On Restricting the Base Component of Transformational Grammars. *Information and Control* (1971), pp. 483–501.

———. "On the Generative Power of Transformational Grammars," *Information Sciences,* pp. 49–83, 1973.

Peters, S. "On Restricting Deletion Transformations." In *The Formal Analysis of Languages,* edited by M. Gross. The Hague: Mouton, 1973.

Putnam, H. "Is Semantics Possible?" In *Languages, Belief and Metaphysics,* edited by H. Kiefer and M. Munitz. Albany: State University of New York Press, 1970.

———. "Some Issues in the Theory of Grammar." In *On Noam Chomsky,* edited by G. Harman. New York: Doubleday, 1974.

Quine, W. V. O. *Word and Object.* Cambridge, Mass.: MIT Press, 1960.

———. *Roots of Reference.* La Salle, Ill.: Open Court, 1974.

Robey, D., ed. *Structuralism: An Introduction.* Oxford: Oxford University Press, 1973.

Searle, J. *Speech Acts.* Cambridge: Cambridge University Press, 1968.

Tarski, A. "The Concept of Truth in Formalized Languages." In

Logic, Semantics, and Metamathematics. Oxford: Oxford University Press, 1956.

VENDLER, Z. *Linguistics in Philosophy.* Ithaca, N.Y.: Cornell University Press, 1967.

———. *Res Cognitans.* Ithaca, N.Y.: Cornell University Press, 1972.

WITTGENSTEIN, L. *Philosophical Remarks.* New York: Barnes and Noble, 1974.

Index

D0103740